The Story

An Interwoven Gospel

By
David Fincher

Publishing and Distribution by
Blue Water Publishing
805 N. Orange Ave.
Fallbrook, CA 92028

www.bluewaterpublishing.biz
www.the-story.biz

ISBN: 978-0-9796160-0-6

Printed by Neyenesch Printers, San Diego, CA

Dedication

To my Lord…

Who bought me with His precious blood
It is Your story I will tell!

How to use this book...

THE STORY was designed to aide any student of the life of Christ in gleaning as much as possible from that wonderful life in a single book setting. One hundred percent of the recorded life of Christ is represented in this book with very few additions. The format is easy to follow and understand.

First, a little background information concerning the interweaving process used in creating this work will be helpful in your utilization of this book. The majority of the text for THE STORY has been taken from the World English Bible (WEB), a public domain revision of the 1901 American Standard Version and the Greek Majority Text. There have been some word exchanges for clarity and poetic beauty.

The chronological account and sequence of events utilized in THE STORY were gathered from both Luke's account of his gospel, (Luke makes it clear in the introduction of his Gospel that it is "in order", Luke 1:3), and the general consensus of scholars concerning the sequence of events in the recorded life of Christ. With that in mind, Luke's Gospel is used as a baseline for the Synoptic Gospels and John's Gospel is inserted in accordance with the majority of Gospel harmonies that deal with the life of Jesus.

There are a number of things to note when reading this book. First, most repetition is eliminated using simple English principles. For instance, if Luke records, "Jesus got into the boat with His disciples" and Matthew says, "Jesus and His disciples got into the boat" then Luke's account is used exclusively. Why? Because both sentences say exactly the same thing even though their sentence structure is slightly different. Hence, the order of priority utilized in the interweaving process concerning the synoptic Gospels was Luke, Matthew, and Mark. In other words, if Luke made a statement and Matthew and Mark made the same statement, then Luke is used. Likewise, if Matthew and Mark are the only Gospels recording an event and Mark's statements are identical to Matthew's, then Matthew's statement is used. John, of course, not being a synoptic Gospel, is placed according to scholarly consensus of the harmonies and in most cases is completely unique. In the few instances when John's statements are identical to the synoptics, he gives way to them in the order stated earlier, Luke, Matthew, then Mark.

The color-coding is very simple and is as follows; Matthew is in Blue, Mark is in Green, Luke is in Purple, and John is in Red. Black words are added text for clarity, conjunction, and/or summary. This color-coding is what makes THE STORY a fantastic tool for the serious student of Christ. One can instantly identify the uniqueness of each writer's account of the Gospels.

This is THE STORY of Christ. It is God's story of His Son. I have simply woven the four accounts of that story into ONE harmonious, complete and exhaustive account of the life that changed the face of history. It is my prayer that as you read THE STORY you will grow in grace and the knowledge of Christ Jesus our Lord and that His amazing life will transform yours into His very own image.

TELL THE STORY!

David Fincher

TABLE OF CONTENTS

LUKE'S REASON FOR WRITING HIS GOSPEL...15

JOHN'S INTRODUCTION 15

JESUS' LEGAL LINEAGE THROUGH JOSEPH
  AND HIS NATURAL LINEAGE THROUGH MARY...16

JOHN'S BIRTH FORETOLD TO ZACHARIAS
JESUS' BIRTH FORETOLD TO MARY
MARY'S VISIT TO ELIZABETH
MARY'S SONG
JOHN'S BIRTH
ZACHARIAS' PROPHETIC SONG...18

JESUS' BIRTH IS EXPLAINED TO JOSEPH 21

THE BIRTH OF JESUS
THE SHEPHERDS ARE TOLD BY ANGELS
JESUS' CIRCUMCISION
JESUS IS PRESENTED AT THE TEMPLE
THE FAMILY RETURNS TO NAZARETH 21

VISIT OF THE MAGI
FLIGHT INTO EGYPT
A NEW HOME IN NAZARETH...23

GROWTH AND EARLY LIFE OF JESUS
JESUS' FIRST PASSOVER IN JERUSALEM
JESUS' YOUTH AND EARLY MANHOOD 24

JOHN THE BAPTIST'S MINISTRY LAUNCHED
JOHN'S PERSON, MESSAGE AND BAPTISM
JOHN'S DESCRIPTION OF CHRIST 25

JESUS' BAPTISM BY JOHN...26

JESUS' TEMPTATION IN THE WILDERNESS 26

JOHN'S SELF-IDENTIFICATION
THE LAMB OF GOD
JESUS' FIRST FOLLOWERS AND FIRST MIRACLE
THE FIRST CLEANSING OF THE TEMPLE
EARLY RESPONSES TO HIS MIRACLES 27

NICODEMUS COMES TO JESUS BY NIGHT
JESUS DECLARES GOD'S LOVE FOR THE WORLD
JOHN'S MINISTRY TO DECREASE 30

JOHN IS ARRESTED AND JESUS DEPARTS JUDEA.................................32

THE SAMARITAN WOMAN
THE SPIRITUAL HARVEST
EVANGELIZATION OF SYCHAR
ARRIVAL IN GALILEE 32

THE GALILEAN MINISTRY
LONG DISTANCE HEALING AT CAPERNAUM...34

MINISTRY AND REJECTION AT NAZARETH 34

MOVE TO CAPERNAUM 35

FIRST CALL OF THE FOUR 36

HEALING OF A DEMONIAC IN THE SYNAGOGUE..36

PETER'S MOTHER-IN-LAW HEALED
MANY HEALINGS 36

TOUR OF GALILEE 37

THE SECOND CALL OF THE FOUR...37

CLEANSING OF A LEPER
MUCH PUBLICITY 38

HEALING OF A PARALYTIC 38

THE CALL OF MATTHEW...39

SUPPER AT MATTHEW'S HOUSE 39

JESUS' PRESENCE CHANGES CONDITIONS...39

A LAME MAN HEALED ON THE SABBATH
AN EFFORT TO KILL JESUS FOR BREAKING THE SABBATH
 AND SAYING HE WAS EQUAL WITH GOD
A DISCOURSE DEMONSTRATING JESUS' EQUALITY WITH GOD 40

CONTROVERSY OVER JESUS' DISCIPLES
PICKING GRAIN ON THE SABBATH DAY 42

A MAN'S WITHERED HAND IS HEALED ON THE SABBATH...........................42

WITHDRAWAL TO THE SEA OF GALILEE
GREAT MULTITUDES FOLLOW JESUS..43

THE TWELVE APOSTLES ARE CHOSEN...43

SETTING FOR THE SERMON ON THE MOUNT..43

THE SERMON ON THE MOUNT...44

The Beatitudes 44

Salt & Light 45

The Fulfillment of the Law..45

Things to Avoid 47

Prayer..47

Treasure on Earth...47

Keeping Your Eye 48

Money...48

Worry..48

Judging...48

Giving 48

Hypocrisy...48

Ask, Seek, & Find...49

Warnings 49

"Lord, Lord" 49

The Wise and Foolish Builders...49

People's Reaction to the Sermon on the Mount...................50

A CENTURION'S FAITH..50

WIDOW'S SON RAISED AT NAIN....................................51

JOHN THE BAPTIST AND THE KINGDOM.....................51

WOES UPON CHORAZIN AND BETHSAIDA
  FOR LACK OF REPENTANCE..52

CHRIST'S FEET ANOINTED BY A REPENTANT WOMAN 52

TOUR WITH THE TWELVE AND OTHER FOLLOWERS 53

BLASPHEMOUS ACCUSATION BY THE PHARISEES 53

AN EVIL GENERATION SEEKS AFTER A SIGN 54

NEW SPIRITUAL TIES 55

THE PARABLE OF THE SOILS...55

THE PARABLE OF THE SEED'S SPONTANEOUS GROWTH 56

THE PARABLE OF THE TARES 57

THE PARABLE OF THE MUSTARD SEED 57

THE PARABLE OF THE LEAVENED LOAF 57

THE PARABLE OF THE TARES EXPLAINED.....................58

THE PARABLE OF THE HIDDEN TREASURE....................58

THE PARABLE OF THE PEARL OF GREAT PRICE 58

THE PARABLE OF THE DRAGNET 58

THE PARABLE OF THE HOUSEHOLDER 58

THE CALMING OF THE STORM 59

GADARENE DEMONIACS HEALED WITH OPPOSITION 59

RETURN TO GALILEE
TOUCHING THE HEM OF THE GARMENT
RAISING OF JAIRUS' DAUGHTER 60

THREE MIRACLES OF HEALING
ANOTHER BLASPHEMOUS ACCUSATION 61

FINAL VISIT TO NAZARETH 61

SHEEP WITHOUT A SHEPHERD
THE PLENTIFUL HARVEST 61

COMMISSIONING OF THE TWELVE 62

WORKERS ARE SENT FORTH 63

HEROD'S MISTAKEN IDENTIFICATION OF JESUS 63

THE EARLIER IMPRISONMENT AND BEHEADING OF JOHN 64

RETURN OF THE WORKERS 64

WITHDRAWAL FROM GALILEE 64

FEEDING THE FIVE THOUSAND 65

AN ATTEMPT TO MAKE JESUS KING 66

JESUS WALKS ON THE WATER 66

GENNESARET HEALINGS 67

THE TRUE BREAD OF LIFE 67

DEFECTION OF SOME DISCIPLES 69

THE TRADITIONS OF MEN 69

GENTILE WOMAN IN TYRE AND SIDON 70

HEALINGS IN DECAPOLIS 71

THE FEEDING OF THE FOUR THOUSAND 72

ANOTHER ENCOUNTER WITH THE SADDUCEES AND PHARISEES ... 72

WARNINGS ABOUT THE PHARISEES, SADDUCEES, AND HERODIANS 72

HEALING OF A BLIND MAN AT BETHSAIDA.......................................73

PETER'S CONFESSION OF CHRIST
FIRST PROPHECY OF THE CHURCH 73

FIRST PREDICTION OF THE CRUCIFIXION AND RESURRECTION 74

THE COMING OF THE SON OF MAN AND JUDGMENT.......................74

THE TRANSFIGURATION OF JESUS 74

ELIJAH AND JOHN THE BAPTIST
THE COMING OF THE SON OF MAN 75

FAITHLESSNESS AND THE HEALING OF A DEMONIC BOY 75

SECOND PREDICTION OF THE RESURRECTION 76

PAYING THE TEMPLE TAX 77

ARGUMENTS OVER GREATNESS 77

WARNINGS AGAINST CAUSING OTHERS TO STUMBLE...................78

FORGIVENESS OF A SINNING BROTHER.......................................78

RIDICULE BY JESUS' HALF-BROTHERS 80

JOURNEY THROUGH SAMARIA...80

COMPLETE COMMITMENT DEMANDED 80

MIXED REACTION TO JESUS' TEACHING AND MIRACLES
A FRUSTRATED ATTEMPT TO ARREST JESUS
THE ADULTERESS WOMAN IS FORGIVEN
THE LIGHT OF THE WORLD
INVITATION TO BELIEVE
ATTEMPTED STONING 81

COMMISSIONING OF THE SEVENTY 85

RETURN OF THE SEVENTY...86

THE GOOD SAMARITAN..86

JESUS VISITS WITH MARY AND MARTHA.......................................87

LESSON ON HOW TO PRAY
PARABLE OF THE IMPORTUNATE FRIEND.....................................87

ANOTHER BLASPHEMOUS ACCUSATION
ANOTHER DEBATE..88

WOES TO THE SCRIBES AND PHARISEES 89

WARNINGS TO THE DISCIPLES ABOUT HYPOCRISY 90

WARNINGS ABOUT GREED AND WEALTH 90

WARNINGS CONCERNING THE SECOND COMING 91

WARNINGS ABOUT COMING DIVISIONS 92

THE SIGNS OF THE TIMES 92

REPENT OR PERISH 92

OPPOSITION FOR HEALING A WOMAN ON THE SABBATH 93

THE HEALING OF THE BLIND MAN 93

THE GOOD SHEPHERD AND THE THIEF 96

MORE DIVISIONS AMONG THE JEWS
ANOTHER ATTEMPT TO ARREST JESUS 96

JESUS GOES BACK ACROSS THE JORDAN 97

QUESTIONS ABOUT SALVATION AND THE KINGDOM 97

JESUS' COMING DEATH AND LAMENT OVER JERUSALEM 98

HEALING OF A MAN WITH DROPSY 98

THE COST OF DISCIPLESHIP 99

THE LOST SHEEP, THE LOST COIN, THE LOST SON 100

THE SHREWD MANAGER 101

THE RICH MAN AND LAZARUS 102

SIN, FAITH, AND DUTY 103

THE SICKNESS AND DEATH OF LAZARUS 103

LAZARUS IS RAISED FROM THE DEAD 104

THE PLOT TO KILL JESUS 105

TEN LEPERS HEALED WHILE PASSING THROUGH SAMARIA 106

MORE ON THE COMING OF THE SON OF MAN 106

PARABLES ON PRAYER 107

DIVORCE AND REMARRIAGE 108

LITTLE CHILDREN AND THE KINGDOM 108

RICHES AND THE KINGDOM 109

PARABLE OF THE VINEYARD 110

THIRD PREDICTION OF THE RESURRECTION 111

A MOTHER'S REQUEST AND AMBITIOUS PRIDE 111

HEALING OF BLIND BARTIMAEUS...112

THE SALVATION OF ZACCHAEUS 112

PARABLE OF THE TEN MINAS 113

ARRIVAL AT BETHANY 114

MARY ANOINTS JESUS' FEET...114

TRIUMPHAL ENTRY INTO JERUSALEM 115

THE CURSING OF THE FIG TREE 116

THE SECOND CLEANSING OF THE TEMPLE 117

JESUS AGAIN PREDICTS HIS DEATH..117

CONTINUED UNBELIEF BY THE JEWS 118

THE WITHERED FIG TREE AND FAITH 118

THE AUTHORITY OF JESUS IS QUESTIONED 119

THE PARABLE OF THE TWO SONS 119

THE PARABLE OF THE TENANTS..120

THE PARABLE OF THE WEDDING BANQUET...121

PAYING TAXES TO CAESAR..121

SADDUCEES QUESTION JESUS...122

THE GREATEST COMMANDMENT...123

WHOSE SON IS CHRIST?...123

WOES TO THE SCRIBES AND PHARISEES 123

LAMENT OVER JERUSALEM..125

THE POOR WIDOW'S GIFT..125

THE DESTRUCTION OF THE TEMPLE FORETOLD
THE DESTRUCTION OF JERUSALEM FORETOLD
THE SECOND COMING FORETOLD..125

PARABLES TEACHING WATCHFULNESS 128

THE JUDGMENT SEAT OF CHRIST..129

THE PLOT AGAINST JESUS INTENSIFIES 130

JUDAS AGREES TO BETRAY JESUS 131

PREPARING THE PASSOVER MEAL 131

THE PASSOVER MEAL BEGINS 131

WASHING THE DISCIPLE'S FEET 131

THE BETRAYER IS IDENTIFIED 132

ARGUMENTS ABOUT GREATNESS 133

THE FIRST PREDICTION OF PETER'S DENIAL 133

THE LORD'S SUPPER IS INSTITUTED 134

JESUS COMFORTS THE DISCIPLES
  AND PROMISES THE HOLY SPIRIT 135

THE VINE AND THE BRANCHES 136

OPPOSITION FROM THE WORLD 137

THE WORK OF THE HOLY SPIRIT 137

GRIEF OF THE DISCIPLES WILL BE TURNED INTO JOY 138

PROMISE OF PEACE 138

JESUS PRAYS FOR HIMSELF,
  HIS DISCIPLES, AND ALL BELIEVERS 139

SECOND PREDICTION OF PETER'S DENIAL 140

JESUS' AGONY IN THE GARDEN 140

JESUS IS BETRAYED, ARRESTED AND FORSAKEN 141

FIRST JEWISH PHASE, BEFORE ANNAS
PETER BEGINS TO DENY JESUS 142

SECOND JEWISH PHASE, BEFORE CAIAPHAS AND THE SANHEDRIN 143

PETER DENIES JESUS 144

THIRD JEWISH PHASE, BEFORE THE SANHEDRIN 144

THE REMORSE AND SUICIDE OF JUDAS 145

FIRST ROMAN PHASE, BEFORE PILATE 145

SECOND ROMAN PHASE, BEFORE HEROD 146

THIRD ROMAN PHASE, BEFORE PILATE AGAIN 147

MOCKERY BY THE ROMAN SOLDIERS 149

JOURNEY TO GOLGOTHA..149

FIRST THREE HOURS ON THE CROSS.................................149

THE LAST THREE HOURS ON THE CROSS.........................151

THE WITNESSES TO JESUS' DEATH.................................151

JESUS' DEATH CONFIRMED AND THE BODY TAKEN DOWN........................152

JESUS' BODY IS PLACED IN THE TOMB............................152

THE GUARD AT THE TOMB...152

THE TOMB IS VISITED BY THE WOMEN............................153

THE STONE IS ROLLED AWAY...153

THE TOMB IS FOUND EMPTY BY THE WOMEN...................153

THE TOMB IS FOUND EMPTY BY PETER AND JOHN..........154

APPEARANCE TO MARY MAGDALENE.............................154

APPEARANCES TO THE OTHER WOMEN.........................155

THE SOLDIER'S REPORT TO THE JEWISH AUTHORITIES.................................155

APPEARANCE ON THE ROAD TO EMMAUS.......................155

THE REPORT BY THE TWO TO THE DISCIPLES.................156

APPEARANCE TO THE TEN DISCIPLES.............................156

APPEARANCE TO THE ELEVEN..157

ANOTHER APPEARANCE TO THE DISCIPLES
PETER IS RESTORED...157

APPEARANCE TO THE ELEVEN IN GALILEE......................159

APPEARANCE TO THE DISCIPLES IN JERUSALEM............159

JESUS BLESSES THE DISCIPLES AND ASCENDS...............160

The Story

An Interwoven Gospel

LUKE'S REASON FOR WRITING HIS GOSPEL
Luke 1:1-4

Since many have undertaken to set in order a narrative concerning those matters which have been fulfilled among us, even as those who from the beginning were eyewitnesses and ministers of the word delivered them to us, it seemed good to me also, having traced the course of all things accurately from the first, to write to you in order, most excellent Theophilus; that you might know the certainty concerning the things in which you were instructed.

JOHN'S INTRODUCTION
John 1:1-18

In the beginning was the Word, and the Word was with God, and the Word was God. The Same was in the beginning with God.

All things were made through Him. Without Him was not anything made that has been made. In Him was life, and the life was the light of men. The light shines in the darkness, and the darkness hasn't overcome it.

There came a man, sent from God, whose name was John. The same came as a witness, that he might testify about the Light, that all might believe through him. He was not the Light, but was sent that he might testify about the Light. The true Light, that enlightens everyone, was coming into the world.

He was in the world, and the world was made through Him, and the world didn't recognize Him. He came to His own, and those who were His own didn't receive Him. But as many as received Him, to them He gave the right to become God's children, to those who believe in His name: who were born not of blood, nor of the will of the flesh, nor of the will of man, but of God.

The Word became flesh, and lived among us. We saw His glory, such glory as of the one and only Son of the Father, full of grace and truth.

John testified about Him. He cried out, saying, "This was He of Whom I said, 'He Who comes after me has surpassed me, for He was before me.'" From His fullness we all received grace upon grace. For the law was given through Moses; grace and truth came through Jesus Christ. No one has seen God at any time. The one and only Son, Who is in the bosom of the Father, He has declared Him.

JESUS' LEGAL LINEAGE THROUGH JOSEPH
AND HIS NATURAL LINEAGE THROUGH MARY
Matthew 1:1-17; Luke 3:23b-38

The book of the generation of Jesus Christ, the son of David, the son of Abraham.

> Abraham became the father of Isaac.
> Isaac became the father of Jacob.
> Jacob became the father of Judah and his brothers.
> Judah became the father of Perez and Zerah by Tamar.
> Perez became the father of Hezron.
> Hezron became the father of Ram.
> Ram became the father of Amminadab.
> Amminadab became the father of Nahshon.
> Nahshon became the father of Salmon.
> Salmon became the father of Boaz by Rahab.
> Boaz became the father of Obed by Ruth.
> Obed became the father of Jesse.
> Jesse became the father of David the king.
> David became the father of Solomon by her who had been the wife of
>   Uriah.
> Solomon became the father of Rehoboam.
> Rehoboam became the father of Abijah.
> Abijah became the father of Asa.
> Asa became the father of Jehoshaphat.
> Jehoshaphat became the father of Joram.
> Joram became the father of Uzziah.
> Uzziah became the father of Jotham.
> Jotham became the father of Ahaz.
> Ahaz became the father of Hezekiah.
> Hezekiah became the father of Manasseh.
> Manasseh became the father of Amon.
> Amon became the father of Josiah.
> Josiah became the father of Jechoniah and his brothers,
>   at the time of the exile to Babylon. After the exile to Babylon,
> Jechoniah became the father of Shealtiel.
> Shealtiel became the father of Zerubbabel.
> Zerubbabel became the father of Abiud.
> Abiud became the father of Eliakim.
> Eliakim became the father of Azor.
> Azor became the father of Sadoc.
> Sadoc became the father of Achim.
> Achim became the father of Eliud.
> Eliud became the father of Eleazar.
> Eleazar became the father of Matthan.
> Matthan became the father of Jacob.

Jacob became the father of Joseph, the husband of Mary,
from whom was born Jesus, who is called Christ.

So all the generations from Abraham to David are fourteen generations; from David to the exile to Babylon fourteen generations; and from the carrying away to Babylon to the Christ, fourteen generations.

Jesus being the son (as was supposed) of Joseph,
  the son of Heli, the son of Matthat,
  the son of Levi, the son of Melchi,
  the son of Jannai, the son of Joseph,
  the son of Mattathias, the son of Amos,
  the son of Nahum, the son of Esli,
  the son of Naggai, the son of Maath,
  the son of Mattathias, the son of Semein,
  the son of Joseph, the son of Judah,
  the son of Joanan, the son of Rhesa,
  the son of Zerubbabel, the son of Shealtiel,
  the son of Neri, the son of Melchi,
  the son of Addi, the son of Cosam,
  the son of Elmodam, the son of Er,
  the son of Josa, the son of Eliezer,
  the son of Jorim, the son of Matthat,
  the son of Levi, the son of Simeon,
  the son of Judah, the son of Joseph,
  the son of Jonan, the son of Eliakim,
  the son of Melea, the son of Menan,
  the son of Mattatha, the son of Nathan,
  the son of David, the son of Jesse,
  the son of Obed, the son of Boaz,
  the son of Salmon, the son of Nahshon,
  the son of Amminadab, the son of Aram,
  the son of Joram, the son of Hezron,
  the son of Perez, the son of Judah,
  the son of Jacob, the son of Isaac,
  the son of Abraham, the son of Terah,
  the son of Nahor, the son of Serug,
  the son of Reu, the son of Peleg,
  the son of Eber, the son of Shelah
  the son of Cainan, the son of Arphaxad,
  the son of Shem, the son of Noah,
  the son of Lamech, the son of Methuselah,
  the son of Enoch, the son of Jared,
  the son of Mahalaleel, the son of Cainan,
  the son of Enos, the son of Seth,
  the son of Adam, the son of God.

JOHN'S BIRTH FORETOLD TO ZACHARIAS
JESUS' BIRTH FORETOLD TO MARY
MARY'S VISIT TO ELIZABETH
MARY'S SONG
JOHN'S BIRTH
ZACHARIAS' PROPHETIC SONG
Luke 1:5-80

There was in the days of Herod, the king of Judea, a certain priest named Zacharias, of the priestly division of Abijah. He had a wife of the daughters of Aaron, and her name was Elizabeth. They were both righteous before God, walking blamelessly in all the commandments and ordinances of the Lord. But they had no child, because Elizabeth was barren, and they both were well advanced in years.

Now it happened, while he executed the priest's office before God in the order of his division, according to the custom of the priest's office, his lot was to enter into the temple of the Lord and burn incense. The whole multitude of the people were praying outside at the hour of incense.

An angel of the Lord appeared to him, standing on the right side of the altar of incense. Zacharias was troubled when he saw him, and fear fell upon him. But the angel said to him, "Don't be afraid, Zacharias, because your request has been heard, and your wife, Elizabeth, will bear you a son, and you shall call his name John. You will have joy and gladness; and many will rejoice at his birth. For he will be great in the sight of the Lord, and he will drink no wine nor strong drink. He will be filled with the Holy Spirit, even from his mother's womb. He will turn many of the children of Israel to the Lord, their God. He will go before Him in the spirit and power of Elijah, 'to turn the hearts of the fathers to the children,' and the disobedient to the wisdom of the just; to make ready a people prepared for the Lord."

Zacharias said to the angel, "How can I be sure of this? For I am an old man, and my wife is well advanced in years."

The angel answered him, "I am Gabriel, who stands in the presence of God. I was sent to speak to you, and to bring you this good news. Behold, you will be silent and not able to speak, until the day that these things will happen, because you didn't believe my words, which will be fulfilled in their proper time."

The people were waiting for Zacharias, and they marveled that he delayed in the temple. When he came out, he could not speak to them, and they perceived that he had seen a vision in the temple. He continued making signs to them, and remained mute.

It happened, when the days of his service were fulfilled, he departed to his house. After these days Elizabeth, his wife, conceived, and she hid herself five months, saying, "Thus has the Lord done to me in the days in which He looked at me, to take away my reproach among men."

Now in the sixth month, the angel Gabriel was sent from God to a city of Galilee, named Nazareth, to a virgin pledged to be married to a man whose name was Joseph, of the house of David. The virgin's name was Mary. Having come in, the angel said to her, "Rejoice, you highly favored one! The Lord is with you. Blessed are you among women!"

But when she saw him, she was greatly troubled at the saying, and considered what kind of salutation this might be. The angel said to her, "Don't be afraid, Mary, for you have found favor with God. Behold, you will conceive in your womb, and bring forth a son, and will call His name 'Jesus.' He will be great, and will be called the Son of the Most High. The Lord God will give Him the throne of His father, David, and He will reign over the house of Jacob forever. There will be no end to His Kingdom."

Mary said to the angel, "How can this be, seeing I am a virgin?"

The angel answered her, "The Holy Spirit will come on you, and the power of the Most High will overshadow you. Therefore also the Holy One Who is born from you will be called the Son of God. Behold, Elizabeth, your relative, also has conceived a son in her old age; and this is the sixth month with her who was called barren. For everything spoken by God is possible."

Mary said, "Behold, the handmaid of the Lord; be it to me according to your word." The angel departed from her.

Mary arose in those days and went into the hill country with haste, into a city of Judah, and entered into the house of Zacharias and greeted Elizabeth. It happened, when Elizabeth heard Mary's greeting, that the baby leaped in her womb, and Elizabeth was filled with the Holy Spirit. She called out with a loud voice, and said, "Blessed are you among women, and blessed is the fruit of your womb! Why am I so favored, that the mother of my Lord should come to me? For behold, when the voice of your greeting came into my ears, the baby leaped in my womb for joy! Blessed is she who believed, for there will be a fulfillment of the things which have been spoken to her from the Lord!"

Mary said,

> "My soul magnifies the Lord.
> My spirit has rejoiced in God my Savior,
>   for He has looked at the humble state of His handmaid.
> For behold, from now on, all generations will call me blessed.
> For He Who is mighty has done great things for me.
> Holy is His name.
> His mercy is for generations of generations
>   on those who fear Him.
> He has shown strength with His arm.
> He has scattered the proud in the imagination of their heart.
> He has put down princes from their thrones.
> And has exalted the lowly.
> He has filled the hungry with good things.
> He has sent the rich away empty.
> He has given help to Israel, His servant,
>   that He might remember mercy,
>   as He spoke to our fathers, To Abraham and his seed forever."

Mary stayed with her about three months, and then returned to her house.

Now the time that Elizabeth should give birth was fulfilled, and she brought forth a son. Her neighbors and her relatives heard that the Lord had magnified His mercy towards her, and they rejoiced with her.

It happened on the eighth day, that they came to circumcise the child; and they would have called him Zacharias, after the name of the father. His mother answered, "Not so; but he will be called John."

They said to her, "There is no one among your relatives who is called by this name."

They made signs to his father, what he would have him called. He asked for a writing tablet, and wrote, "His name is John." They all marveled. His mouth was opened immediately, and his tongue freed, and he spoke, blessing God. Fear came on all who lived around them, and all these sayings were talked about throughout all the hill country of Judea. All who heard them laid them up in their heart, saying, "What then will this child be?" The hand of the Lord was with him.

His father, Zacharias, was filled with the Holy Spirit, and prophesied, saying,

> "Blessed be the Lord, the God of Israel,
>   for He has visited and worked redemption for His people;
>   and has raised up a horn of salvation
>   for us in the house of His servant David
>   (as He spoke by the mouth of His holy prophets
>   who have been from of old),
>   salvation from our enemies, and from the hand of all who hate us;
>   to show mercy towards our fathers,
>   to remember His holy covenant,
>   the oath which He spoke to Abraham, our father,
>   to grant to us that we, being delivered out of the hand of our enemies,
>   should serve Him without fear,
>   in holiness and righteousness before Him all the days of our life.
> And you, child, will be called a prophet of the Most High,
>   for you will go before the face of the Lord to make ready His ways,
>   to give knowledge of salvation to His people by the remission of their
>   sins, because of the tender mercy of our God,
>   whereby the dawn from on high will visit us,
>   to shine on those who sit in darkness and the shadow of death;
>   to guide our feet into the way of peace."

The child was growing, and becoming strong in spirit, and was in the desert until the day of his public appearance to Israel.

JESUS' BIRTH IS EXPLAINED TO JOSEPH
Matthew 1:18-25

Now the birth of Jesus Christ was like this; for after His mother, Mary, was engaged to Joseph, before they came together, she was found to be with child by the Holy Spirit. Joseph, her husband, being a righteous man, and not willing to make her a public example, intended to divorce her secretly.

But when he thought about these things, behold, an angel of the Lord appeared to him in a dream, saying, "Joseph, son of David, don't be afraid to take to yourself Mary, your wife, for that which is conceived in her is of the Holy Spirit. She shall bring forth a son. You shall call His name Jesus, for it is He Who shall save His people from their sins."

Now all this has happened, that it might be fulfilled which was spoken by the Lord through the prophet, saying,

"Behold, the virgin shall be with child, and shall bring forth a son.
They shall call His name Immanuel;"

Which is, being interpreted, "God with us."

Joseph arose from his sleep, and did as the angel of the Lord commanded him, and took his wife to himself; and didn't know her sexually until she had brought forth her firstborn son. He named Him Jesus.

THE BIRTH OF JESUS
THE SHEPHERDS ARE TOLD BY ANGELS
JESUS' CIRCUMCISION
JESUS IS PRESENTED AT THE TEMPLE
THE FAMILY RETURNS TO NAZARETH
Luke 2:1-39

Now it happened in those days, that a decree went out from Caesar Augustus that all the world should be enrolled. This was the first enrollment made when Quirinius was governor of Syria. All went to enroll themselves, everyone to his own city.

Joseph also went up from Galilee, out of the city of Nazareth, into Judea, to the city of David, which is called Bethlehem, because he was of the house and family of David; to enroll himself with Mary, who was pledged to be married to him as wife, being with child. It happened, while they were there, that the day had come that she should give birth. She brought forth her firstborn son, and she wrapped Him in swaddling clothes, and laid Him in a manger, because there was no room for them in the inn.

There were shepherds in the same country staying in the field, and keeping watch by night over their flock. Behold, an angel of the Lord stood by them, and the glory of the Lord shone around them, and they were terrified. The angel said to them, "Don't be afraid, for behold, I bring you good news of great joy which will be to all the people. For there is born to you, this day, in the city of David, a Savior, Who is Christ the Lord. This is the sign to you: you will find a baby wrapped in swaddling clothes, lying in a manger."

Suddenly, there was with the angel a multitude of the Heavenly host praising God, and saying,

"Glory to God in the highest,
on earth peace, good will toward men."

It happened, when the angels went away from them into the Heaven, that the shepherds said one to another, "Let's go to Bethlehem, now, and see this thing that has happened, which the Lord has made known to us."

They came with haste, and found both Mary and Joseph, and the baby was lying in the feeding trough. When they saw it, they publicized widely the saying which was spoken to them about this child. All who heard it wondered at the things which were spoken to them by the shepherds. But Mary kept all these sayings, pondering them in her heart. The shepherds returned, glorifying and praising God for all the things that they had heard and seen, just as it was told them.

When eight days were fulfilled for the circumcision of the child, His name was called Jesus, which was given by the angel before He was conceived in the womb.

When the days of their purification according to the law of Moses were fulfilled, they brought Him up to Jerusalem, to present Him to the Lord as it is written in the law of the Lord,

"Every male who opens the womb shall be called holy to the Lord,"

and to offer a sacrifice according to that which is said in the law of the Lord,

"A pair of turtledoves, or two young pigeons."

Behold, there was a man in Jerusalem whose name was Simeon. This man was righteous and devout, looking for the consolation of Israel, and the Holy Spirit was on him. It had been revealed to him by the Holy Spirit that he should not see death before he had seen the Lord's Christ. He came in the Spirit into the temple. When the parents brought in the child, Jesus, that they might do concerning Him according to the custom of the law, then he received Him into his arms, and blessed God, and said, "Now You are releasing your servant, Master, according to Your word, in peace; For my eyes have seen Your salvation, which You have prepared before the face of all peoples; A light for revelation to the Gentiles, and the glory of Your people Israel."

Joseph and His mother were marveling at the things which were spoken concerning Him, and Simeon blessed them, and said to Mary, His mother, "Behold, this child is set for the falling and the rising of many in Israel, and for a sign which is spoken against. Yes, a sword will pierce through your own soul, that the thoughts of many hearts may be revealed."

There was one Anna, a prophetess, the daughter of Phanuel, of the tribe of Asher (she was of a great age, having lived with a husband seven years from her virginity, and she had been a widow for about eighty-four years), who didn't depart from the temple, worshipping with fastings and petitions night and day. Coming up at that very hour, she gave thanks to the Lord, and spoke of Him to all those who were looking for redemption in Jerusalem.

When they had accomplished all things that were according to the law of the Lord, they returned into Galilee, to their own city, Nazareth.

VISIT OF THE MAGI
FLIGHT INTO EGYPT
A NEW HOME IN NAZARETH
Matthew 2:1-23

Now when Jesus was born in Bethlehem of Judea in the days of Herod the king, behold, wise men from the east came to Jerusalem, saying, "Where is He Who is born King of the Jews? For we saw His star in the east, and have come to worship Him."

When Herod the king heard it, he was troubled, and all Jerusalem with him. Gathering together all the Chief Priests and Scribes of the people, he asked them where the Christ would be born. They said to him, "In Bethlehem of Judea, for thus it is written through the prophet,

'You Bethlehem, land of Judah,
are in no way least among the princes of Judah:
for out of you shall come forth a governor,
who shall shepherd My people, Israel.'"

Then Herod secretly called the wise men, and learned from them exactly what time the star appeared. He sent them to Bethlehem, and said, "Go and search diligently for the young child. When you have found Him, bring me word, so that I also may come and worship Him."

They, having heard the king, went their way; and behold, the star, which they saw in the east, went before them, until it came and stood over where the young child was. When they saw the star, they rejoiced with exceedingly great joy. They came into the house and saw the young child with Mary, His mother, and they fell down and worshiped Him. Opening their treasures, they offered to Him gifts: gold, frankincense, and myrrh. Being warned in a dream that they shouldn't return to Herod, they went back to their own country another way.

Now when they had departed, behold, an angel of the Lord appeared to Joseph in a dream, saying, "Arise and take the young child and His mother, and flee into Egypt, and stay there until I tell you, for Herod will seek the young child to destroy Him."

He arose and took the young child and His mother by night, and departed into Egypt, and was there until the death of Herod; that it might be fulfilled which was spoken by the Lord through the prophet, saying,

"Out of Egypt I called My son."

Then Herod, when he saw that he was mocked by the wise men, was exceedingly angry, and sent out, and killed all the male children who were in Bethlehem and in all the surrounding countryside, from two years old and under, according to the exact time which he had learned from the wise men. Then that which was spoken by Jeremiah the prophet was fulfilled, saying,

"A voice was heard in Ramah,
lamentation, weeping and great mourning,
Rachel weeping for her children;
she wouldn't be comforted,
because they are no more."

But when Herod was dead, behold, an angel of the Lord appeared in a dream to Joseph in Egypt, saying, "Arise and take the young child and His mother, and go into the land of Israel, for those who sought the young child's life are dead."

He arose and took the young child and His mother, and came into the land of Israel. But when he heard that Archelaus was reigning over Judea in the place of his father, Herod, he was afraid to go there. Being warned in a dream, he withdrew into the region of Galilee, and came and lived in a city called Nazareth; that it might be fulfilled which was spoken through the prophets:

"He will be called a Nazarene."

GROWTH AND EARLY LIFE OF JESUS
JESUS' FIRST PASSOVER IN JERUSALEM
JESUS' YOUTH AND EARLY MANHOOD
Luke 2:40-52

The child Jesus was growing, and was becoming strong in Spirit, being filled with wisdom, and the grace of God was upon Him.

His parents went every year to Jerusalem at the feast of the Passover. When He was twelve years old, they went up to Jerusalem according to the custom of the feast, and when they had fulfilled the days, as they were returning, the boy Jesus stayed behind in Jerusalem. Joseph and His mother didn't know it, but supposing Him to be in the company, they went a day's journey, and they looked for Him among their relatives and acquaintances. When they didn't find Him, they returned to Jerusalem, looking for Him. It happened after three days they found Him in the temple, sitting in the midst of the teachers, both listening to them, and asking them questions. All who heard Him were amazed at His understanding and His answers. When they saw Him, they were astonished, and His mother said to Him, "Son, why have You treated us this way? Behold, Your father and I were anxiously looking for You."

He said to them, "Why were you looking for Me? Didn't you know that I must be in My Father's house?" They didn't understand the saying which He spoke to them.

And He went down with them, and came to Nazareth. He was subject to them, and His mother kept all these sayings in her heart. And Jesus increased in wisdom and stature, and in favor with God and men.

JOHN THE BAPTIST'S MINISTRY LAUNCHED
JOHN'S PERSON, MESSAGE AND BAPTISM
JOHN'S DESCRIPTION OF CHRIST
Matthew 3:1-12; Mark 1:1-8; Luke 3:1-18

The beginning of the gospel of Jesus Christ, the Son of God.

Now in the fifteenth year of the reign of Tiberius Caesar, Pontius Pilate being governor of Judea, and Herod being tetrarch of Galilee, and his brother Philip tetrarch of the region of Ituraea and Trachonitis, and Lysanias tetrarch of Abilene, in the high priesthood of Annas and Caiaphas, the word of God came to John, the son of Zacharias, in the wilderness.

In those days, John the Baptist came, preaching in the wilderness of Judea, saying, "Repent, for the Kingdom of Heaven is at hand!" He came into all the region around the Jordan, preaching the baptism of repentance for remission of sins. For this is He Who was spoken of and as it is written in the book of the words of Isaiah the prophet, and in the prophets,

"Behold, I send My messenger before Your face,
   who will prepare Your way before You.
The voice of one crying in the wilderness,
   'Make ready the way of the Lord. Make His paths straight.
Every valley will be filled. Every mountain and hill will be brought low.
The crooked will become straight, and the rough ways smooth.
All flesh will see God's salvation.'"

John said therefore to the multitudes when he saw many of the Pharisees and Sadducees who went out to be baptized by him, "You offspring of vipers, who warned you to flee from the wrath to come? Bring forth therefore fruits worthy of repentance, and don't begin to say or think to yourselves, 'We have Abraham for our father;' for I tell you that God is able to raise up children to Abraham from these stones! Even now the axe also lies at the root of the trees. Every tree therefore that doesn't bring forth good fruit is cut down, and thrown into the fire."

Now John himself wore clothing made of camel's hair, with a leather belt around his waist. His food was locusts and wild honey. Then people from Jerusalem, all of Judea, and all the region around the Jordan went out to him. They were baptized by him in the Jordan, confessing their sins.

The multitudes asked him, "What then must we do?"

He answered them, "He who has two coats, let him give to him who has none. He who has food, let him do likewise."

Tax collectors also came to be baptized, and they said to him, "Teacher, what must we do?"

He said to them, "Collect no more than that which is appointed to you."

Soldiers also asked him, saying, "What about us? What must we do?"

He said to them, "Extort from no one by violence, neither accuse anyone wrongfully. Be content with your wages."

As the people were in expectation, and all men reasoned in their hearts concerning John, whether perhaps he was the Christ, John answered them all, "I indeed baptize you with water, but there is One Who comes Who is mightier than I, the latchet of Whose sandals I am not worthy to stoop down and loosen. He will baptize you in the Holy Spirit and fire, Whose fan is in His hand, and He will thoroughly cleanse His threshing floor, and will gather the wheat into His barn; but He will burn up the chaff with unquenchable fire." Then with many other exhortations he preached good news to the people.

JESUS' BAPTISM BY JOHN
Matthew 3:13-17; Mark 1:9-11; Luke 3:21-23a

It happened in those days, when all the people were baptized, that Jesus came from Nazareth of Galilee to the Jordan and to John, to be baptized by him. But John would have hindered Him, saying, "I need to be baptized by You, and You come to me?"

But Jesus, answering, said to him, "Allow it now, for this is the fitting way for us to fulfill all righteousness." Then he allowed Him.

Now it happened, when Jesus also had been baptized, He went up directly from the water and as He was praying the heavens were opened, and the Holy Spirit descended in a bodily form as a dove on Him; and a voice came out of Heaven, saying, "You are My beloved Son. In You I am well pleased." Jesus Himself, when He began to teach, was about thirty years old.

JESUS' TEMPTATION IN THE WILDERNESS
Matthew 4:1-11; Mark 1:12-13; Luke 4:1-13

Jesus, full of the Holy Spirit, returned from the Jordan, and was led by the Spirit into the wilderness for forty days. He was with the wild animals; being tempted by the devil, by Satan himself. He ate nothing in those days, (He had fasted forty days and forty nights). Afterward, when they were completed, He was hungry.

The tempter came and the devil said to Him, "If You are the Son of God, command this stone to become bread."

Jesus answered him, saying, "It is written,

> 'Man shall not live by bread alone,
> but by every word that proceeds out of the mouth of God.'"

Again, the devil, leading Him up on an exceedingly high mountain, showed Him all the kingdoms of the world and their glory in a moment of time. The devil said to Him, "I will give You all this authority and all of these things, and their glory, for it has been delivered to me; and I give it to whomever I want. If You therefore will worship before me, it will all be Yours."

Jesus answered him, "Get behind Me Satan! For it is written,

> 'You shall worship the Lord your God, and Him only shall you serve.'"

He led Him to Jerusalem, and set Him on the pinnacle of the temple, and said to Him, "If You are the Son of God, cast Yourself down from here, for it is written,

> 'He will give His angels charge concerning You, to guard You;' and,
> 'On their hands they will bear You up, lest perhaps
> You dash Your foot against a stone.'"

Jesus answering, said to him, "Again, it is written and it has been said,

> 'You shall not tempt the Lord your God.'"

When the devil had completed every temptation, he departed from Him until another time and behold, angels came and ministered to Him.

JOHN'S SELF-IDENTIFICATION
THE LAMB OF GOD
FIRST FOLLOWERS AND FIRST MIRACLE
THE FIRST CLEANSING OF THE TEMPLE
EARLY RESPONSES TO HIS MIRACLES
John 1:19-2:25

This is John's testimony, when the Jews sent priests and Levites from Jerusalem to ask him, "Who are you?"

He confessed, and didn't deny, but he confessed, "I am not the Christ."

They asked him, "What then? Are you Elijah?"

He said, "I am not."

"Are you the Prophet?"

He answered, "No."

They said therefore to him, "Who are you? Give us an answer to take back to those who sent us. What do you say about yourself?"

He said, "I am the voice of one crying in the wilderness,

'Make straight the way of the Lord,'

as Isaiah the prophet said."

The ones who had been sent were from the Pharisees and asked him, "Why then do you baptize, if you are not the Christ, nor Elijah, nor the Prophet?"

John answered them, "I baptize in water, but among you stands One Whom you don't know. He is the One Who comes after me, Who is preferred before me, Whose sandal strap I'm not worthy to loosen."

These things were done in Bethany beyond the Jordan, where John was baptizing.

The next day, he saw Jesus coming to him, and said, "Behold, the Lamb of God, Who takes away the sin of the world! This is He of Whom I said, 'After me comes a man Who is preferred before me, for He was before me.' I didn't know Him, but for this reason I came baptizing in water: that He would be revealed to Israel."

John testified, saying, "I have seen the Spirit descending like a dove out of Heaven, and it remained on Him. I didn't recognize Him, but He Who sent me to baptize in water, He said to me, 'On Whomever you will see the Spirit descending, and remaining on Him, the same is He Who baptizes in the Holy Spirit.' I have seen, and have testified that this is the Son of God."

Again, the next day, John was standing with two of his disciples, and he looked at Jesus as He walked, and said, "Behold, the Lamb of God!"

The two disciples heard him speak, and they followed Jesus. Jesus turned, and saw them following, and said to them, "What are you looking for?"

They said to Him, "Rabbi" (which is to say, being interpreted, Teacher), "where are You staying?"

He said to them, "Come, and see."

They came and saw where He was staying, and they stayed with Him that day. It was about the tenth hour.

One of the two who heard John, and followed Jesus, was Andrew, Simon Peter's brother. He first found his own brother, Simon, and said to him, "We have found the Messiah!" (which is, being interpreted, Christ). He brought him to Jesus.

Jesus looked at him, and said, "You are Simon the son of Jonah. You shall be called Cephas" (which is by interpretation, Peter).

On the next day, He was determined to go out into Galilee, and He found Philip. Jesus said to him, "Follow Me."

Now Philip was from Bethsaida, of the city of Andrew and Peter. Philip found Nathanael, and said to him, "We have found Him, of Whom Moses in the law, and the prophets, wrote: Jesus of Nazareth, the son of Joseph."

Nathanael said to him, "Can any good thing come out of Nazareth?"

Philip said to him, "Come and see."

Jesus saw Nathanael coming to Him, and said about him, "Behold, an Israelite indeed, in whom is no deceit!"

Nathanael said to Him, "How do You know me?"

Jesus answered him, "Before Philip called you, when you were under the fig tree, I saw you."

Nathanael answered Him, "Rabbi, You are the Son of God! You are King of Israel!"

Jesus answered him, "Because I told you, 'I saw you underneath the fig tree,' do you believe? You will see greater things than these!" He said to him, "Most assuredly, I tell you, hereafter you will see Heaven opened, and the angels of God ascending and descending on the Son of Man."

The third day, there was a marriage in Cana of Galilee. Jesus' mother was there. Jesus also was invited, with His disciples, to the marriage. When the wine ran out, Jesus' mother said to Him, "They have no wine."

Jesus said to her, "Woman, what does that have to do with you and Me? My hour has not yet come."

His mother said to the servants, "Whatever He says to you, do it."

Now there were six water pots of stone set there after the Jews' manner of purifying, containing twenty to thirty gallons apiece.

Jesus said to them, "Fill the water pots with water." They filled them up to the brim.

He said to them, "Now draw some out, and take it to the ruler of the feast."

So they took it. When the ruler of the feast tasted the water now become wine, and didn't know where it came from (but the servants who had drawn the water knew), the ruler of the feast called the bridegroom, and said to him,

"Everyone serves the good wine first, and when the guests have drunk freely, then that which is worse. You have kept the good wine until now!"

This beginning of His signs Jesus did in Cana of Galilee, and revealed His glory; and His disciples believed in Him.

After this, He went down to Capernaum, He, and His mother, His brothers, and His disciples; and they stayed there a few days.

The Passover of the Jews was at hand, and Jesus went up to Jerusalem. He found in the temple those who sold oxen, sheep, and doves, and the changers of money sitting. He made a whip of cords, and threw all out of the temple, both the sheep and the oxen; and He poured out the changer's money, and overthrew their tables. To those who sold the doves, He said, "Take these things out of here! Don't make My Father's house a marketplace!"

His disciples remembered that it was written,

"Zeal for Your house will eat Me up."

The Jews therefore answered Him, "What sign do You show us, seeing that You do these things?"

Jesus answered them, "Destroy this temple, and in three days I will raise it up."

The Jews therefore said, "Forty-six years was this temple in building, and will You raise it up in three days?" But He spoke of the temple of His body. When therefore He was raised from the dead, His disciples remembered that He said this, and they believed the Scripture, and the word which Jesus had said.

Now when He was in Jerusalem at the Passover, during the feast, many believed in His name, observing His signs which He did. But Jesus didn't trust Himself to them, because He knew everyone, and because He didn't need for anyone to testify concerning man; for He Himself knew what was in man.

NICODEMUS COMES TO JESUS BY NIGHT
JESUS DECLARES GOD'S LOVE FOR THE WORLD
JOHN'S MINISTRY TO DECREASE
John 3:1-36

Now there was a man of the Pharisees named Nicodemus, a ruler of the Jews. The same came to Him by night, and said to Him, "Rabbi, we know that You are a teacher come from God, for no one can do these signs that You do, unless God is with Him."

Jesus answered him, "Most assuredly, I tell you, unless one is born again, he can't see the Kingdom of God."

Nicodemus said to Him, "How can a man be born when he is old? Can he enter a second time into his mother's womb, and be born?"

Jesus answered, "Most assuredly I tell you, unless one is born of water and spirit, he can't enter into the Kingdom of God! That which is born of the flesh is flesh. That which is born of the Spirit is spirit. Don't marvel that I said to you, 'You must be born again.' The wind blows where it wants to, and you hear its sound, but don't know where it comes from and where it is going. So is everyone who is born of the Spirit."

Nicodemus answered Him, "How can these things be?"

Jesus answered him, "Are you the teacher of Israel, and don't understand these things? Most assuredly I tell you, We speak that which We know, and testify of that which We have seen, and you don't receive Our witness. If I told you earthly things and you don't believe, how will you believe if I tell you Heavenly things? No one has ascended into Heaven, but He Who descended out of Heaven, the Son of Man, Who is in Heaven. As Moses lifted up the serpent in the wilderness, even so must the Son of Man be lifted up, that whoever believes in Him should not perish, but have eternal life.

For God so loved the world, that He gave His One and only Son, that whoever believes in Him should not perish, but have eternal life. For God didn't send His Son into the world to judge the world, but that the world should be saved through Him. He who believes in Him is not judged. He who doesn't believe has been judged already, because he has not believed in the name of the only born Son of God. This is the judgment, that the light has come into the world, and men loved the darkness rather than the light; for their works were evil. For everyone who does evil hates the light, and doesn't come to the light, lest his works would be exposed. But he who does the truth comes to the light, that his works may be revealed, that they have been done in God."

After these things, Jesus came with His disciples into the land of Judea. He stayed there with them, and baptized. John also was baptizing in Enon near Salim, because there was much water there. They came, and were baptized. For John was not yet thrown into prison. There arose therefore a questioning on the part of John's disciples with some Jews about purification. They came to John, and said to him, "Rabbi, He Who was with you beyond the Jordan, to Whom you have testified, behold, the same baptizes, and everyone is coming to Him."

John answered, "A man can receive nothing, unless it has been given him from Heaven. You yourselves testify that I said, 'I am not the Christ,' but, 'I have been sent before Him.' He who has the bride is the bridegroom; but the friend of the bridegroom, who stands and hears him, rejoices greatly because of the bridegroom's voice. This, my joy, therefore is made full. He must increase, but I must decrease.

He Who comes from above is above all. He who is from the earth belongs to the earth, and speaks of the earth. He Who comes from Heaven is above all. What He has seen and heard, of that He testifies; and no one receives His witness. He who has received His witness has set His seal to this, that God is true. For He Whom God has sent speaks the words of God; for God gives the Spirit without measure. The Father loves the Son, and has given all things into His hand. One who believes in the Son has eternal life, but one who disobeys the Son won't see life, but the wrath of God remains on him."

31

JOHN IS ARRESTED AND JESUS DEPARTS JUDEA
Matthew 4:12; Mark 1:14a; Luke 3:19-20,4:14a; John 4:1-4

Herod the tetrarch, being reproved by him for Herodias, his brother's wife, and for all the evil things which Herod had done, added this also to them all, that he shut up John in prison.

Now when Jesus heard that John was delivered up and was taken into custody and also when the Lord knew that the Pharisees had heard that Jesus was making and baptizing more disciples than John (although Jesus Himself didn't baptize, but His disciples), He left Judea and withdrew into Galilee in the power of the Spirit.

As He returned into Galilee, He needed to pass through Samaria.

THE SAMARITAN WOMAN
THE SPIRITUAL HARVEST
EVANGELIZATION OF SYCHAR
ARRIVAL IN GALILEE
John 4:5-45

So He came to a city of Samaria, called Sychar, near the parcel of ground that Jacob gave to his son, Joseph. Jacob's well was there. Jesus therefore, being tired from His journey, sat down by the well. It was about the sixth hour.

A woman of Samaria came to draw water. Jesus said to her, "Give Me a drink." For His disciples had gone away into the city to buy food.

The Samaritan woman therefore said to Him, "How is it that You, being a Jew, ask for a drink from me, a Samaritan woman?" (For Jews have no dealings with Samaritans.)

Jesus answered her, "If you knew the gift of God, and Who it is Who says to you, 'Give Me a drink,' you would have asked Him, and He would have given you living water."

The woman said to Him, "Sir, You have nothing to draw with, and the well is deep. From where then have You that living water? Are You greater than our father, Jacob, who gave us the well, and drank of it himself, as did his children, and his cattle?"

Jesus answered her, "Everyone who drinks of this water will thirst again, but whoever drinks of the water that I will give him will never thirst again; but the water that I will give him will become in him a well of water springing up to eternal life."

The woman said to Him, "Sir, give me this water, so that I don't get thirsty, neither come all the way here to draw."

Jesus said to her, "Go, call your husband, and come here."

The woman answered, "I have no husband."

Jesus said to her, "You said well, 'I have no husband,' for you have had five husbands; and he whom you now have is not your husband. This you have said truly."

The woman said to Him, "Sir, I perceive that You are a prophet. Our fathers worshiped in this mountain, and you Jews say that in Jerusalem is the place where people ought to worship."

Jesus said to her, "Woman, believe Me, the hour comes, when neither in this mountain, nor in Jerusalem, will you worship the Father. You worship that which you don't know. We worship that which we know; for salvation is from the Jews. But the hour comes, and now is, when the true worshippers will worship the Father in spirit and truth, for the Father seeks such to be His worshippers. God is Spirit, and those who worship Him must worship in spirit and truth."

The woman said to Him, "I know the Messiah comes," (He Who is called Christ). "When He has come, He will declare to us all things."

Jesus said to her, "I am He, the One Who speaks to you."

At this, His disciples came. They marveled that He was speaking with a woman; yet no one said, "What are you looking for?" or, "Why do You speak with her?"

So the woman left her water pot, and went away into the city, and said to the people, "Come, see a man Who told me everything that I did. Can this be the Christ?" They went out of the city, and were coming to Him.

In the meanwhile, the disciples urged Him, saying, "Rabbi, eat."

But He said to them, "I have food to eat that you don't know about."

The disciples therefore said one to another, "Has anyone brought Him something to eat?"

Jesus said to them, "My food is to do the will of Him Who sent Me, and to accomplish His work. Don't you say, 'There are yet four months until the harvest?' Behold, I tell you, lift up your eyes, and look at the fields, that they are white for harvest already. He who reaps receives wages, and gathers fruit to eternal life; that both he who sows and he who reaps may rejoice together. For in this the saying is true,

> 'One sows, and another reaps.'

"I sent you to reap that for which you haven't labored. Others have labored, and you have entered into their labor."

From that city many of the Samaritans believed in Him because of the word of the woman, who testified, "He told me everything that I did." So when the Samaritans came to Him, they begged Him to stay with them. He stayed there two days. Many more believed because of His word.

They said to the woman, "Now we believe, not because of your speaking; for we have heard for ourselves, and know that this is indeed the Christ, the Savior of the world."

After the two days He went out from there and went into Galilee. For Jesus Himself testified that a prophet has no honor in his own country. So when He came into Galilee, the Galileans received Him, having seen all the things that He did in Jerusalem at the feast, for they also went to the feast.

THE GALILEAN MINISTRY
LONG DISTANCE HEALING AT CAPERNAUM
Matthew 4:17; Mark 1:14b-15; Luke 4:14b-15; John 4:46-54

Jesus came therefore again to Cana of Galilee where He made the water into wine and news about Him spread through all the surrounding area. He taught in their synagogues, being glorified by all. From that time, Jesus began to preach the gospel of the Kingdom of God, and to say, "The time is fulfilled, and the Kingdom of God is at hand! Repent! For the Kingdom of Heaven is at hand. Repent, and believe in the gospel."

There was a certain nobleman whose son was sick at Capernaum. When he heard that Jesus had come out of Judea into Galilee, he went to Him, and begged Him that He would come down and heal his son, for he was at the point of death.

Jesus therefore said to him, "Unless you see signs and wonders, you will in no way believe."

The nobleman said to Him, "Sir, come down before my child dies."

Jesus said to him, "Go your way. Your son lives."

The man believed the word that Jesus spoke to him, and he went his way. As he was now going down, his servants met him and reported, saying "Your child lives!" So he inquired of them the hour when he began to get better. They said therefore to him, "Yesterday at the seventh hour, the fever left him." So the father knew that it was at that hour in which Jesus said to him, "Your son lives." He believed, as did his whole house.

This is again the second sign that Jesus did, having come out of Judea into Galilee.

MINISTRY AND REJECTION AT NAZARETH
Luke 4:16-31

He came to Nazareth, where He had been brought up. He entered, as was His custom, into the synagogue on the Sabbath day, and stood up to read. The book of the prophet Isaiah was handed to Him. He opened the book, and found the place where it was written,

> "The Spirit of the Lord is on Me, because He has anointed Me to
>   preach good news to the poor.
> He has sent Me to heal the brokenhearted,
>   to proclaim release to the captives,
>   recovering of sight to the blind,
>   to deliver those who are crushed,
>   and to proclaim the acceptable year of the Lord."

He closed the book, gave it back to the attendant, and sat down. The eyes of all in the synagogue were fastened on Him. He began to tell them, "Today, this Scripture has been fulfilled in your hearing."

All testified about Him, and wondered at the gracious words which proceeded out of His mouth, and they said, "Isn't this Joseph's son?"

He said to them, "Doubtless you will tell Me this parable, 'Physician, heal Yourself! Whatever we have heard done at Capernaum, do also here in Your hometown.'"

He said, "Most assuredly I tell you, no prophet is acceptable in his hometown. But truly I tell you, there were many widows in Israel in the days of Elijah, when heaven was shut up three years and six months, when a great famine came over all the land. Elijah was sent to none of them, except to Zarephath, in the land of Sidon, to a woman who was a widow. There were many lepers in Israel in the time of Elisha the prophet, yet not one of them was cleansed, except Naaman, the Syrian."

They were all filled with wrath in the synagogue, as they heard these things. They rose up, threw Him out of the city, and led Him to the brow of the hill that their city was built on, that they might throw Him off the cliff. But He, passing through the midst of them, went His way.

He came down to Capernaum, a city of Galilee. He was teaching them on the Sabbath day.

MOVE TO CAPERNAUM
Matthew 4:13-16

Leaving Nazareth, He came and lived in Capernaum, which is by the sea, in the region of Zebulun and Naphtali, that it might be fulfilled which was spoken through Isaiah the prophet, saying,

> "The land of Zebulun and the land of Naphtali,
>   toward the sea, beyond the Jordan,
>   Galilee of the Gentiles,
>   the people who sat in darkness saw a great light,
>   to those who sat in the region and shadow of death,
>   to them light has dawned."

FIRST CALL OF THE FOUR
Matthew 4:18-22; Mark 1:16-20

Walking by the sea of Galilee, He saw two brothers: Simon, who is called Peter, and Andrew, his brother, casting a net into the sea; for they were fishermen. He said to them, "Come after Me, and I will make you into fishers for men."

They immediately left their nets and followed Him.

Going on a little further from there, He saw two other brothers, James the son of Zebedee, and John his brother, in the boat with Zebedee their father, mending their nets. Immediately He called them.

They immediately left the boat and their father with the hired servants, and followed Him.

HEALING OF A DEMONIAC IN THE SYNAGOGUE
Mark 1:21-28; Luke 4:31b-37

They went into Capernaum, and immediately on the Sabbath day He entered into the synagogue and taught and they were astonished at His teaching, for His word was with authority and not as the Scribes.

Immediately there was in the synagogue a man who had a spirit of an unclean demon, and he cried out with a loud voice, saying, "Ah! what have we to do with You, Jesus of Nazareth, Jesus, You Nazarene? Have You come to destroy us? I know You, Who You are: the Holy One of God!"

Jesus rebuked him, saying, "Be silent, and come out of him!"

When the demon had convulsed him and thrown him down in their midst and crying with a loud voice, he came out of him, having done him no harm.

Amazement came on all, so that they questioned among themselves and they spoke together, one with another, saying, "What is this word? What is this? A new teaching? For with authority and power He commands even the unclean spirits, and they obey Him and come out!"

News about Him went out immediately into every place and all the region of Galilee and the surrounding region.

PETER'S MOTHER-IN-LAW HEALED
MANY HEALINGS
Matthew 8:14-17; Mark 1:29-34; Luke 4:38-41

He rose up from the synagogue, and entered into Simon's and Andrew's house with James and John.

Simon's mother-in-law was afflicted and lay sick with a great fever, and immediately they told Him about her and they begged Him for her. He stood over her, He touched her hand and took her by the hand, raised her up, rebuked the fever; and it left her. Immediately she rose up and served them.

When the sun was setting and evening came, all those who had any sick with various diseases brought them to Him; and He laid His hands on every one of them, and healed them. All the city was gathered together at the door. He cast out the spirits with a word and the demons also came out from many, crying out, and saying, "You are the Christ, the Son of God!" Rebuking them, He didn't allow them to speak, because they knew that He was the Christ. All this was done that it might be fulfilled which was spoken through Isaiah the prophet, saying:

"He took our infirmities, and bore our diseases."

TOUR OF GALILEE
Matthew 4:23-24; Mark 1:35-39; Luke 4:42-44

And in the morning, rising up a great while before day, He departed and went into an uninhabited place and prayed there. Simon and those who were with Him followed after Him; and they found Him, and told Him, "Everyone is looking for You." The multitudes looked for Him, and came to Him, and held on to Him, so that He wouldn't go away from them. But He said to them, "I must preach the good news of the Kingdom of God to the other cities also. For this reason I have been sent and I came forth."

Jesus went about in all Galilee preaching and teaching in the synagogues. He was preaching the gospel of the Kingdom, and healing every disease and every sickness among the people and casting out demons. The report about Him went out into all Syria. They brought to Him all who were sick, afflicted with various diseases and torments, possessed with demons, epileptics, and paralytics; and He healed them.

THE SECOND CALL OF THE FOUR
Luke 5:1-11

Now it happened, while the multitude pressed on Him and heard the word of God, that He was standing by the lake of Gennesaret. He saw two boats standing by the lake, but the fishermen had gone out of them, and were washing their nets. He entered into one of the boats, which was Simon's, and asked him to put out a little from the land. He sat down and taught the multitudes from the boat.

When He had finished speaking, He said to Simon, "Put out into the deep, and let down your nets for a catch."

Simon answered Him, "Master, we worked all night, and took nothing; but at Your word I will let down the net."

When they had done this, they caught a great multitude of fish, and their net was breaking. They beckoned to their partners in the other boat, that they should come and help them. They came, and filled both boats, so that they began to sink.

But Simon Peter, when he saw it, fell down at Jesus' knees, saying, "Depart from me, for I am a sinful man, Lord." For he was amazed, and all who were with him, at the catch of fish which they had caught; and so also were James and John, sons of Zebedee, who were partners with Simon.

Jesus said to Simon, "Don't be afraid. From now on you will catch men." When they had brought their boats to land, they left everything, and followed Him.

CLEANSING OF A LEPER
MUCH PUBLICITY
Matthew 8:2-4; Mark 1:40-45; Luke 5:12-16

It happened, while He was in one of the cities, behold, there was a man full of leprosy. When he saw Jesus, he knelt down to Him fell on his face and worshiped Him, and begged Him, saying, "Lord, if You want to, You can make me clean."

Being moved with compassion, He stretched out His hand, and touched him, saying, "I want to. Be made clean."

Immediately the leprosy left him and he was cleansed.

He strictly warned him and charged him saying, "See that you tell no one, but go your way, and show yourself to the priest, and offer for your cleansing according to what Moses commanded, for a testimony to them."

But he went out, and began to proclaim it much, and to spread about the matter, so that Jesus could no more openly enter into a city, but was outside in desert places: and they came to Him from everywhere. The report concerning Him spread much more, and great multitudes came together to hear, and to be healed by Him of their infirmities. But He withdrew Himself into the desert, and prayed.

HEALING OF A PARALYTIC
Matthew 9:1-8; Mark 2:1-12; Luke 5:17-26

He entered into a boat, and crossed over, and came into His own city. When He entered again into Capernaum after some days, it was heard that He was in the house. It happened on one of those days, that He was teaching and immediately many were gathered together, so that there was no more room, not even around the door; and He spoke the word to them. There were Pharisees and teachers of the law sitting by, who had come out of every village of Galilee, Judea, and Jerusalem. The power of the Lord was with Him to heal the sick. Behold, four men brought a paralyzed man on a cot, and they sought to bring him in to lay before Jesus. Not finding a way to bring him in because of the multitude, they went up to the house-top, they removed the roof where He was and when they had broken it up, they let him down through the tiles with his cot into the midst before Jesus.

Jesus, seeing their faith, said to him, "Man, Son, cheer up! Your sins are forgiven you."

The Scribes and the Pharisees began to reason to themselves and in their hearts, saying, "Who is this that speaks blasphemies? Why does this man speak blasphemies like that? Who can forgive sins, but God alone?"

But Jesus, immediately perceiving in His Spirit and knowing their thoughts, answered them, "Why are you reasoning so in your hearts? Why do you think evil in your hearts? Which is easier to say, 'Your sins are forgiven you,' or to say, 'Arise and take up your bed, and walk?' But that you may know that the Son of Man has authority on earth to forgive sins" (He said to the paralyzed man), "I tell you, arise, and take up your cot, and go to your house." Immediately he rose up before them, and took up that which he was laying on, and departed to his house, glorifying God. Amazement took hold on all, and they glorified God. They were filled with fear, saying, "We have seen strange things today and we never saw anything like this!"

THE CALL OF MATTHEW
Matthew 9:9; Mark 2:13-14; Luke 5:27-28

After these things He went out again by the seaside. All the multitude came to Him, and He taught them.

As Jesus passed by from there, He saw a tax collector named Matthew, Levi, the son of Alphaeus, sitting at the tax office, and said to him, "Follow Me!" He left everything, and rose up and followed Him.

SUPPER AT MATTHEW'S HOUSE
Matthew 9:10-13; Mark 2:15-17; Luke 5:29-32

Levi made a great feast for Him in his house. It happened as He sat in the house, there was a great crowd of tax collectors, sinners, and others who were reclining with them and they sat down with Jesus and His disciples for there were many, and they followed Him. When the Pharisees saw it, along with the Scribes, they murmured against His disciples, saying, "Why do you and your Teacher eat and drink with the tax collectors and sinners?"

When Jesus heard it, He answered them, "Those who are healthy have no need for a physician, but those who are sick do. But you go and learn what this means: 'I desire mercy, and not sacrifice,' for I have not come to call the righteous, but sinners to repentance."

JESUS' PRESENCE CHANGES CONDITIONS
Matthew 9:14-17; Mark 2:18-22; Luke 5:33-39

John's disciples and the Pharisees were fasting and they came and asked Him, "Why do John's disciples often fast and pray, likewise also the disciples of the Pharisees, but Yours eat and drink?"

He said to them, "Can you make the friends of the bridegroom fast or mourn while the bridegroom is with them? As long as they have the bridegroom with them, they can't fast. But the days will come when the bridegroom will be taken away from them. Then they will fast in those days."

He also told a parable to them. "No one puts a piece from a new unshrunk garment on an old garment, for the patch would tear away from the garment, and it will tear the new, and a worse hole is made, and also the piece from the new will not match the old. No one puts new wine into old wineskins, or else the new wine will burst the skins, and it will be spilled, and the skins will be destroyed. But new wine must be put into fresh wineskins, and both are preserved. No man having drunk old wine immediately desires new, for he says, 'The old is better.'"

A LAME MAN HEALED ON THE SABBATH
AN EFFORT TO KILL JESUS FOR BREAKING THE SABBATH
AND SAYING HE WAS EQUAL WITH GOD
A DISCOURSE DEMONSTRATING JESUS' EQUALITY WITH GOD
John 5:1-47

After these things, there was a feast of the Jews, and Jesus went up to Jerusalem. Now in Jerusalem by the sheep gate, there is a pool, which is called in Hebrew, "Bethesda," having five porches. In these lay a great multitude of those who were sick, blind, lame, or paralyzed, waiting for the moving of the water; for an angel of the Lord went down at certain times into the pool, and stirred up the water. Whoever stepped in first after the stirring of the water was made whole of whatever disease he had. A certain man was there, who had been sick for thirty-eight years. When Jesus saw him lying there, and knew that he had been sick for a long time, He asked him, "Do you want to be made well?"

The sick man answered Him, "Sir, I have no one to put me into the pool when the water is stirred up, but while I'm coming, another steps down before me."

Jesus said to him, "Arise, take up your mat, and walk." Immediately, the man was made well, and took up his mat and walked.

Now it was the Sabbath on that day. So the Jews said to him who was cured, "It is the Sabbath. It is not lawful for you to carry the mat."

He answered them, "He Who made me well, the same said to me, 'Take up your mat, and walk.'"

Then they asked him, "Who is the man Who said to you, 'Take up your mat, and walk'?"

But he who was healed didn't know Who it was, for Jesus had withdrawn, a crowd being in the place.

Afterward Jesus found him in the temple, and said to him, "Behold, you are made well. Sin no more, so that nothing worse happens to you." The man went away, and told the Jews that it was Jesus Who had made him well.

For this cause the Jews persecuted Jesus, and sought to kill Him, because He did these things on the Sabbath. But Jesus answered them, "My Father is still working, so I am working, too." For this cause therefore the Jews sought all the more to kill Him, because He not only broke the Sabbath, but also called God His own Father, making Himself equal with God.

Jesus therefore answered them, "Most assuredly, I tell you, the Son can do nothing of Himself, but what He sees the Father doing. For whatever things He does, these the Son also does likewise. For the Father loves the Son, and shows Him all things that He Himself does. He will show Him greater works than these, that you may marvel. For as the Father raises the dead and gives them life, even so the Son also gives life to whom He desires. For the Father judges no one, but He has given all judgment to the Son, that all may honor the Son, even as they honor the Father. He who doesn't honor the Son doesn't honor the Father Who sent Him.

"Most assuredly I tell you, he who hears My word, and believes Him Who sent Me, has eternal life, and doesn't come into judgment, but has passed out of death into life. Most assuredly, I tell you, the hour comes, and now is, when the dead will hear the Son of God's voice; and those who hear will live. For as the Father has life in Himself, even so He gave to the Son also to have life in Himself. He also gave Him authority to execute judgment, because He is a Son of Man.

"Don't marvel at this, for the hour comes, in which all that are in the tombs will hear His voice, and will come out; those who have done good, to the resurrection of life; and those who have done evil, to the resurrection of judgment. I can of Myself do nothing. As I hear, I judge, and My judgment is righteous; because I don't seek My own will, but the will of My Father Who sent Me.

"If I testify about Myself, My witness is not valid. It is another who testifies about Me. I know that the testimony which He testifies about Me is true.

"You have sent to John, and he has testified to the truth. But the testimony which I receive is not from man. However, I say these things that you may be saved. He was the burning and shining lamp, and you were willing to rejoice for a while in his light.

"But the testimony which I have is greater than that of John, for the works which the Father gave Me to accomplish, the very works that I do, testify about Me, that the Father has sent Me. The Father Himself, Who sent Me, has testified about Me. You have neither heard His voice at any time, nor seen His form. You don't have His word living in you; because you don't believe Him Whom He sent.

"You search the Scriptures, because you think that in them you have eternal life; and these are they which testify about Me. Yet you will not come to Me, that you may have life.

"I don't receive glory from men. But I know you, that you don't have God's love in yourselves. I have come in My Father's name, and you don't receive Me. If another comes in his own name, you will receive him. How can you believe, who receive glory from one another, and you don't seek the glory that comes from the only God?

"Don't think that I will accuse you to the Father. There is one who accuses you, even Moses, on whom you have set your hope. For if you believed Moses, you would believe Me; for he wrote about Me. But if you don't believe his writings, how will you believe My words?"

CONTROVERSY OVER JESUS' DISCIPLES
PICKING GRAIN ON THE SABBATH DAY
Matthew 12:1-8; Mark 2:23-28; Luke 6:1-5

Now it happened on the second Sabbath after the first, that He was going through the grain fields. His disciples were hungry and as they went, plucked the heads of grain, and ate, rubbing them in their hands. But some of the Pharisees said to Jesus and His disciples, "Behold, Your disciples do what is not lawful to do on the Sabbath. Why do you do that which is not lawful to do on the Sabbath day?"

Jesus, answering them, said, "Haven't you read what David did when he had need and when he was hungry, he, and those who were with him; how he entered into the house of God when Abiathar was high priest, and took and ate the show bread, and gave also to those who were with him, which is not lawful to eat except for the priests alone? Or have you not read in the law, that on the Sabbath day, the priests in the temple profane the Sabbath, and are guiltless? But I tell you that one greater than the temple is here. But if you had known what this means, 'I desire mercy, and not sacrifice,' you would not have condemned the guiltless."

He said to them, "The Sabbath was made for man, not man for the Sabbath. Therefore the Son of Man is Lord of the Sabbath."

A MAN'S WITHERED HAND IS HEALED ON THE SABBATH
Matthew 12:9-14; Mark 3:1-6; Luke 6:6-11

It also happened on another Sabbath that He entered into the synagogue and taught. There was a man there, and his right hand was withered. The Scribes and the Pharisees watched Him, to see whether He would heal on the Sabbath. They asked Him, "Is it lawful to heal on the Sabbath day?" They said this that they might find an accusation against Him.

But He knew their thoughts; and He said to the man who had the withered hand, "Rise up, and stand in the middle." He arose and stood.

Then Jesus said to them, "I will ask you something: Is it lawful on the Sabbath to do good, or to do harm? To save a life, or to kill? What man is there among you, who has one sheep, and if this one falls into a pit on the Sabbath day, won't he grab on to it, and lift it out? Of how much more value then is a man than a sheep! Therefore it is lawful to do good on the Sabbath day." But they were silent.

When He looked around at them all with anger, being grieved at the hardening of their hearts, He then said to the man, "Stretch out your hand." He did, and his hand was restored whole as sound and healthy as the other. But the Pharisees went out and they were filled with rage, and talked with one another and conspired with the Herodians against Him, how they might destroy Him.

WITHDRAWAL TO THE SEA OF GALILEE
GREAT MULTITUDES FOLLOW JESUS
Matthew 12:15-21 & 4:25; Mark 3:7-12

Jesus, perceiving that they were conspiring to kill Him, withdrew from there to the sea with His disciples. Great multitudes followed Him from Galilee, Decapolis, from Judea, from Jerusalem, from Idumaea, beyond the Jordan, and those from around Tyre and Sidon. He spoke to His disciples that a little boat should stay near Him because of the crowd, so that they wouldn't press on Him. For He had healed many, so that as many as had diseases pressed on Him that they might touch Him. The unclean spirits, whenever they saw Him, fell down before Him, and cried, "You are the Son of God!" He sternly warned them that they should not make Him known.

A great multitude, hearing what great things He did, came to Him and He healed them all, and charged them that they should not make Him known: that it might be fulfilled which was spoken through Isaiah the prophet, saying,

> "Behold, My servant Whom I have chosen;
>   My beloved in Whom My soul is well pleased:
>   I will put My Spirit on Him.
> He will proclaim justice to the Gentiles.
> He will not strive, nor shout;
>   neither will anyone hear His voice in the streets.
> He won't break a bruised reed.
> He won't quench a smoking flax,
>   until He leads justice to victory.
> In His name, the Gentiles will hope."

THE TWELVE APOSTLES ARE CHOSEN
Mark 3:13-19; Luke 6:12-16

It happened in these days, that He went out to the mountain and then He went up into the mountain to pray, and He continued all night in prayer to God. When it was day, He called His disciples, and from them He chose twelve whom He wanted, whom He also named apostles. He appointed these twelve, that they might be with Him, and that He might send them out to preach, and to have authority to heal sicknesses and to cast out demons: Simon, whom He also named Peter; Andrew, his brother; James, the son of Zebedee; John, the brother of James; and he surnamed them Boanerges, which means, Sons of Thunder; Philip; Bartholomew; Matthew; Thomas; James, the son of Alphaeus; Simon, who was called the Zealot; Judas, the son of James who is also called Thaddaeus; and Judas Iscariot, who also became a traitor. He afterwards came into a house.

SETTING FOR THE SERMON ON THE MOUNT
Matthew 5:1-2a; Luke 6:17-19

He came down with them, and stood on a level place, with a crowd of His disciples, and a great number of the people from all Judea and Jerusalem, and the sea coast of Tyre and Sidon, who came to hear Him and to be healed of their diseases; as well as those who were troubled by unclean spirits, and they were being healed. All the multitude sought to touch Him, for power came out from Him and healed them all.

Seeing the multitudes, He went **back** up onto the mountain. When He had sat down, His disciples came to Him.

THE SERMON ON THE MOUNT
Matthew 5:2b-7:29; Luke 6:17-49

The Beatitudes

He lifted up His eyes to His disciples, and He opened His mouth and taught them, saying,

"Blessed are you who are poor,
> For yours is the Kingdom of God.

"Blessed are the poor in spirit,
> For theirs is the Kingdom of Heaven.

"Blessed are those who mourn,
> For they shall be comforted.

"Blessed are the meek,
> For they shall inherit the earth.

"Blessed are you who hunger now and thirst after righteousness,
> For you will be filled.

"Blessed are you who weep now,
> For you will laugh.

"Blessed are the merciful,
> For they shall obtain mercy.

"Blessed are the pure in heart,
> For they shall see God.

"Blessed are the peacemakers,
> For they shall be called children of God.

"Blessed are those who have been persecuted for righteousness' sake,
> For theirs is the Kingdom of Heaven.

"Blessed are you when men shall hate you, when people reproach you, and when they shall exclude and mock you, and throw out your name as evil, and say all kinds of evil against you falsely, for the Son of Man's sake. Rejoice in that day, be exceedingly glad and leap for joy, for behold, your reward is great in Heaven, for their fathers did the same thing to the prophets.

"But woe to you who are rich!
    For you have received your consolation.

"Woe to you, you who are full now!
    For you will be hungry.

"Woe to you who laugh now!
    For you will mourn and weep.

"Woe, when men speak well of you!
    For their fathers did the same thing to the false prophets."

Salt & Light

"You are the salt of the earth, but if the salt has lost its flavor, with what will it be salted? It is then good for nothing, but to be cast out and trodden under the feet of men.

"You are the light of the world. A city set on a hill can't be hidden. Neither do men light a lamp, and put it under a measuring basket, but on a stand; and it shines to all who are in the house. Even so, let your light shine before men; that they may see your good works, and glorify your Father Who is in Heaven.

The Fulfillment of the Law

"Don't think that I came to destroy the law or the prophets. I didn't come to destroy, but to fulfill. For most assuredly, I tell you, until heaven and earth pass away, not even one smallest letter or one tiny pen stroke shall in any way pass away from the law, until all things are accomplished. Whoever, therefore, shall break one of these least commandments, and teach others to do so, shall be called least in the Kingdom of Heaven; but whoever shall do and teach them shall be called great in the Kingdom of Heaven. For I tell you that unless your righteousness exceeds that of the Scribes and Pharisees, there is no way you will enter into the Kingdom of Heaven.

"You have heard that it was said to them of old, 'You shall not murder;' and 'Whoever shall murder shall be in danger of the judgment.' But I tell you, that everyone who is angry with his brother without a cause shall be in danger of the judgment; and whoever shall say to his brother, 'Raca!' shall be in danger of the council; and whoever shall say, 'You fool!' shall be in danger of the fire of Gehenna.

"If therefore you are offering your gift at the altar, and there remember that your brother has anything against you, leave your gift there before the altar, and go your way. First be reconciled to your brother, and then come and offer your gift. Agree with your adversary quickly, while you are with him in the way; lest perhaps the prosecutor deliver you to the judge, and the judge deliver you to the officer, and you be cast into prison. Most assuredly I tell you, you shall by no means get out of there, until you have paid the last penny.

"You have heard that it was said, 'You shall not commit adultery;' but I tell you that everyone who gazes at a woman to lust after her has committed adultery with her already in his heart. If your right eye causes you to stumble, pluck it out and throw it away from you. For it is profitable for you that one of your members should perish, than for your whole body to be cast into Gehenna. If your right hand causes you to stumble, cut it off, and throw it away from you: for it is profitable for you that one of your members should perish, and not your whole body be thrown into Gehenna.

"It was also said, 'Whoever shall divorce his wife, let him give her a certificate of divorce,' but I tell you that whoever divorces his wife, except for the cause of sexual immorality, makes her an adulteress; and whoever marries her when she is divorced commits adultery.

"Again you have heard that it was said to them of old time, 'You shall not make false vows, but shall perform to the Lord your vows,' but I tell you, don't swear at all: neither by Heaven, for it is the throne of God; nor by the earth, for it is the footstool of His feet; nor by Jerusalem, for it is the city of the great King. Neither shall you swear by your head, for you can't make one hair white or black. But let your 'Yes' be 'Yes' and your 'No' be 'No.' Whatever is more than these is of the evil one.

"You have heard that it was said, 'An eye for an eye, and a tooth for a tooth.' But I tell you who hear: love your enemies, do good to those who hate you, bless those who curse you, and pray for those who mistreat you. I tell you, don't resist him who is evil; to him who strikes you on the cheek, offer also the other; and from him who sues you to take away your cloak, don't withhold your coat also. Whoever compels you to go one mile, go with him two. Give to everyone who asks you, and don't turn away him who desires to borrow from you and don't ask him who takes away your goods to give them back again.

"If you love those who love you, what credit or reward is that to you? For even sinners love those who love them. If you do good to those who do good to you, what credit is that to you? For even sinners and the tax collectors do the same. If you lend to those from whom you hope to receive, what credit is that to you? Even sinners lend to sinners, to receive back as much. If you only greet your friends, what more do you do than others? Don't even the tax collectors do the same? Therefore you shall be perfect, just as your Father in Heaven is perfect.

"You have heard that it was said, 'You shall love your neighbor, and hate your enemy.' But I tell you, love your enemies, bless those who curse you, and do good to those who hate you, and lend, expecting nothing back; and pray for those who mistreat you and persecute you, and your reward will be great, and you will be children of your Father Who is in Heaven, children of the Most High; for He is kind toward the unthankful and evil. He makes His sun to rise on the evil and the good, and sends rain on the just and the unjust. Therefore be merciful, even as your Father is also merciful.

Things to Avoid

"Be careful that you don't do your charitable giving before men, to be seen by them, or else you have no reward from your Father Who is in Heaven.

"Therefore when you do merciful deeds, don't sound a trumpet before yourself, as the hypocrites do in the synagogues and in the streets, that they may get glory from men. Most assuredly I tell you, they have received their reward. But when you do merciful deeds, don't let your left hand know what your right hand does, so that your merciful deeds may be in secret, then your Father Who sees in secret will reward you openly.

Prayer

"When you pray, you shall not be as the hypocrites, for they love to stand and pray in the synagogues and in the corners of the streets, that they may be seen by men. Most assuredly, I tell you, they have received their reward. But you, when you pray, enter into your inner chamber, and having shut your door, pray to your Father Who is in secret, and your Father Who sees in secret will reward you openly. In praying, don't use vain repetitions, as the Gentiles do; for they think that they will be heard for their much speaking. Therefore don't be like them, for your Father knows what things you need, before you ask Him.

"Pray like this:

'Our Father in Heaven, may Your name be kept holy.
Let Your Kingdom come.
Let Your will be done, as in Heaven, so on earth.
Give us today our daily bread.
Forgive us our debts, as we also forgive our debtors.
Bring us not into temptation, but deliver us from the evil one.
For Yours is the Kingdom, the power, and the glory forever. Amen.'

"For if you forgive men their trespasses, your Heavenly Father will also forgive you. But if you don't forgive men their trespasses, neither will your Father forgive your trespasses.

"Moreover when you fast, don't be like the hypocrites, with sad faces. For they disfigure their faces, that they may be seen by men to be fasting. Most assuredly I tell you, they have received their reward. But you, when you fast, anoint your head, and wash your face; so that you are not seen by men to be fasting, but by your Father Who is in secret, and your Father, Who sees in secret, will reward you.

Treasure on Earth

"Don't lay up treasures for yourselves on the earth, where moth and rust consume, and where thieves break through and steal; but lay up for yourselves treasures in Heaven, where neither moth nor rust consume, and where thieves don't break through and steal; for where your treasure is, there your heart will be also.

Keeping Your Eye

"The lamp of the body is the eye. If therefore your eye is sound, your whole body will be full of light. But if your eye is evil, your whole body will be full of darkness. If therefore the light that is in you is darkness, how great is the darkness!

Money

"No one can serve two masters, for either he will hate the one and love the other; or else he will be devoted to one and despise the other. You can't serve both God and money. Therefore, I tell you, don't be anxious for your life: what you will eat, or what you will drink; nor yet for your body, what you will wear. Isn't life more than food, and the body more than clothing? See the birds of the sky, that they don't sow, neither do they reap, nor gather into barns. Your Heavenly Father feeds them. Aren't you of much more value than they?

Worry

"Which of you, by being anxious, can add one cubit to the measure of his life? Why are you anxious about clothing? Consider the lilies of the field, how they grow. They don't toil, neither do they spin, yet I tell you that even Solomon in all his glory was not dressed like one of these. But if God so clothes the grass of the field, which today exists, and tomorrow is thrown into the oven, won't He much more clothe you, you of little faith?

"Therefore don't be anxious, saying, 'What will we eat?', 'What will we drink?' or, 'With what will we be clothed?' For the Gentiles seek after all these things, for your Heavenly Father knows that you need all these things. But seek first the Kingdom of God, and His righteousness; and all these things will be given to you as well. Therefore don't be anxious for tomorrow, for tomorrow will be anxious for itself. Each day's own evil is sufficient.

Judging

"Don't judge, and you won't be judged. Don't condemn, and you won't be condemned. Set free, and you will be set free. For with whatever judgment you judge, you will be judged.

Giving

"Give, and it will be given to you: good measure, pressed down, shaken together, and running over, will be given to you. For with the same measure you measure it will be measured back to you."

Hypocrisy

He spoke a parable to them. "Can the blind guide the blind? Won't they both fall into a pit? A disciple is not above his teacher, but everyone when he is fully trained will be like his teacher. Why do you see the speck of chaff that is in your brother's eye, but don't consider the beam that is in your own eye? Or how can you tell your brother, 'Brother, let me remove the speck of chaff that is in your eye,' when you yourself don't see the beam that is in your own eye? You hypocrite! First remove the beam from your own eye, and then you can see clearly to remove the speck of chaff that is in your brother's eye.

"Don't give that which is holy to the dogs, neither throw your pearls before the pigs, lest perhaps they trample them under their feet, and turn and tear you to pieces.

Ask, Seek, & Find

"Ask, and it will be given you. Seek, and you will find. Knock, and it will be opened for you. For everyone who asks receives. He who seeks finds. To him who knocks it will be opened. Or who is there among you, who, if his son asks him for bread, will give him a stone? Or if he asks for a fish, who will give him a serpent? If you then, being evil, know how to give good gifts to your children, how much more will your Father Who is in Heaven give good things to those who ask Him! Therefore as you would like people to do to you, do exactly so to them for this is the law and the prophets.

"Enter in by the narrow gate; for wide is the gate and broad is the way that leads to destruction, and many are those who enter in by it. For narrow is the gate, and straight is the way that leads to life! Few are those who find it.

Warnings

"Beware of false prophets, who come to you in sheep's clothing, but inwardly are ravening wolves. By their fruits you will know them. For there is no good tree that brings forth rotten fruit; nor again a rotten tree that brings forth good fruit. For each tree is known by its own fruit. For people don't gather figs from thorns, nor do they gather grapes from a bramble bush. Every tree that doesn't grow good fruit is cut down, and thrown into the fire. Even so, the good man out of the good treasure of his heart brings out that which is good, and the evil man out of the evil treasure of his heart brings out that which is evil, for out of the abundance of the heart, his mouth speaks. Therefore, by their fruits you will know them.

"Lord, Lord"

"Why do you call Me, 'Lord, Lord,' and do not the things which I say? Not everyone who says to Me, 'Lord, Lord,' will enter into the Kingdom of Heaven; but he who does the will of My Father Who is in Heaven. Many will say to Me in that day, 'Lord, Lord, didn't we prophesy in Your name, in Your name cast out demons, and in Your name do many mighty works?' Then I will tell them, 'I never knew you. Depart from Me, you who work iniquity.'

The Wise and Foolish Builders

"Everyone therefore who comes to Me, and hears My words, and does them, I will show you who he is like. He is like a wise man building a house, who dug and went deep, and laid a foundation on the rock. When a flood arose, the stream broke against that house, and could not shake it, because it was founded on the rock. But he who hears, and doesn't do, is like a foolish man who built a house on the earth without a foundation, against which the stream broke, and immediately it fell, and the ruin of that house was great."

People's Reaction to the Sermon on the Mount

It happened, when Jesus had finished saying these things, that the multitudes were astonished at His teaching, for He taught them with authority, and not like the Scribes.

A CENTURION'S FAITH
Matthew 8:1,5-13; Luke 7:1-10

After He had finished speaking in the hearing of the people, He came down from the mountain and great multitudes followed Him. When He came into Capernaum, a certain centurion's servant, who was dear to him, was sick and at the point of death. When he heard about Jesus, he sent to Him Elders of the Jews, asking Him to come and save his servant. When they came to Jesus, they begged Him earnestly, saying, "He is worthy for You to do this for him, for he loves our nation, and he built our synagogue for us." Jesus went with them.

When He was now not far from the house, the centurion sent friends to Him, and then he himself came saying to Him, "Lord, my servant lies in the house paralyzed, grievously tormented."

Jesus said to him, "I will come and heal him."

The Centurion replied, "But don't trouble Yourself, for I am not worthy for You to come under my roof. Therefore I didn't even think myself worthy to come to You; but just say the word, and my servant will be healed. For I also am a man placed under authority, having under myself soldiers. I tell this one, 'Go!' and he goes; and to another, 'Come!' and he comes; and to my servant, 'Do this,' and he does it."

When Jesus heard these things, He marveled at him, and turned and said to the multitude who followed Him, "Most assuredly I tell you, I have not found such great faith, no, not even in Israel. I tell you that many will come from the east and the west, and will sit down with Abraham, Isaac, and Jacob in the Kingdom of Heaven, but the children of the Kingdom will be thrown out into the outer darkness. There will be weeping and the gnashing of teeth."

Jesus said to the centurion, "Go your way. Let it be done for you as you have believed." His servant was healed in that hour.

Those who were sent, returning to the house, found that the servant who had been sick was well.

WIDOW'S SON RAISED AT NAIN
Luke 7:11-17

It happened soon afterwards, that He went to a city called Nain. Many of His disciples, along with a great multitude, went with Him. Now when He drew near to the gate of the city, behold, one who was dead was carried out, the only son of his mother, and she was a widow. Many people of the city were with her. When the Lord saw her, He had compassion on her, and said to her, "Don't cry."

He came near and touched the coffin, and the bearers stood still. He said, "Young man, I tell you, arise!" He who was dead sat up, and began to speak. And He gave him to his mother.

Fear took hold of all, and they glorified God, saying, "A great prophet has arisen among us!" and, "God has visited His people!" This report went out concerning Him in the whole of Judea, and in all the surrounding region.

JOHN THE BAPTIST AND THE KINGDOM
Matthew 11:2-19; Luke 7:18-35

The disciples of John told him about all these things. Now when John heard in the prison the works of Christ, he called to himself two of his disciples, sent them to Jesus, saying, "Are You the One Who is coming, or should we look for another?" When the men had come to Him, they said, "John the Baptist has sent us to You, saying, 'Are You He Who comes, or should we look for another?'"

In that hour He cured many of diseases and plagues and evil spirits; and to many who were blind He gave sight. Jesus answered them, "Go and tell John the things which you have seen and heard: that the blind receive their sight, the lame walk, the lepers are cleansed, the deaf hear, the dead are raised up, and the poor have good news preached to them. Blessed is he who is not offended by Me and finds no occasion for stumbling in Me."

When John's messengers had departed, He began to tell the multitudes about John, "What did you go out into the wilderness to see? A reed shaken by the wind? But what did you go out to see? A man clothed in soft clothing? Behold, those who are gorgeously dressed and wear soft clothing and live delicately, are in kings' courts. But what did you go out to see? A prophet? Yes, I tell you, and much more than a prophet. This is he of whom it is written,

> 'Behold, I send My messenger before Your face,
> who will prepare Your way before You.'

"For most assuredly I tell you, among those who are born of women there is not a greater prophet than John the Baptist, yet he who is least in the Kingdom of God and the Kingdom of Heaven is greater than he. From the days of John the Baptist until now, the Kingdom of Heaven suffers violence, and the violent take it by force. For all the prophets and the law prophesied until John. If you are willing to receive it, this is Elijah, who is to come. He who has ears to hear, let him hear."

When all the people and the tax collectors heard this, they declared God to be just, having been baptized with John's baptism. But the Pharisees and the Lawyers rejected the counsel of God, not being baptized by him themselves.

But the Lord said, "To what then will I liken the people of this generation? What are they like? They are like children who sit in the marketplace, and call one to another, saying, 'We piped the flute to you, and you didn't dance. We mourned for you, and you didn't weep.'

"For John the Baptist came neither eating bread nor drinking wine, and you say, 'He has a demon.' The Son of Man has come eating and drinking, and you say, 'Behold, a gluttonous man, and a drunkard; a friend of tax collectors and sinners!' Wisdom is justified by all her children."

WOES UPON CHORAZIN AND BETHSAIDA
FOR LACK OF REPENTANCE
Matthew 11:20-30

Then He began to denounce the cities in which most of His mighty works had been done, because they didn't repent. "Woe to you, Chorazin! Woe to you, Bethsaida! For if the mighty works had been done in Tyre and Sidon which were done in you, they would have repented long ago in sackcloth and ashes. But I tell you, it will be more tolerable for Tyre and Sidon on the day of judgment than for you. You, Capernaum, who are exalted to Heaven, you will go down to Hades. For if the mighty works had been done in Sodom which were done in you, it would have remained until this day. But I tell you that it will be more tolerable for the land of Sodom, on the day of judgment, than for you."

At that time, Jesus answered, "I thank You, Father, Lord of Heaven and earth, that You hid these things from the wise and understanding, and revealed them to infants. Yes, Father, for so it was well-pleasing in Your sight.

"All things have been delivered to Me by My Father. No one knows the Son, except the Father; neither does anyone know the Father, except the Son, and he to whom the Son desires to reveal Him.

"Come to Me, all you who labor and are heavily burdened, and I will give you rest. Take My yoke upon you, and learn from Me, for I am gentle and lowly in heart; and you will find rest for your souls. For My yoke is easy, and My burden is light."

CHRIST'S FEET ANOINTED BY A REPENTANT WOMAN
Luke 7:36-50

One of the Pharisees invited Him to eat with him. He entered into the Pharisee's house, and sat at the table. Behold, a woman in the city who was a sinner, when she knew that He was reclining in the Pharisee's house, she brought an alabaster jar of ointment. Standing behind Him at His feet weeping, she began to wet His feet with her tears, and she wiped them with the hair of her head, kissed His feet, and anointed them with the ointment.

Now when the Pharisee who had invited Him saw it, he said to himself, "This man, if He were a prophet, would have perceived who and what kind of woman this is who touches Him, that she is a sinner."

Jesus answered him, "Simon, I have something to tell you."

He said, "Teacher, say on."

"A certain lender had two debtors. The one owed five hundred denarii, and the other fifty. When they couldn't pay, he forgave them both. Which of them therefore will love him most?"

Simon answered, "He, I suppose, to whom he forgave the most."

He said to him, "You have judged correctly."

Turning to the woman, He said to Simon, "Do you see this woman? I entered into your house, and you gave Me no water for My feet, but she has wet My feet with her tears, and wiped them with the hair of her head. You gave Me no kiss, but she, since the time I came in, has not ceased to kiss My feet. You didn't anoint My head with oil, but she has anointed My feet with ointment. Therefore I tell you, her sins, which are many, are forgiven, for she loved much. But to whom little is forgiven, the same loves little."

He said to her, "Your sins are forgiven."

Those who sat at the table with Him began to say to themselves, "Who is this Who even forgives sins?"

He said to the woman, "Your faith has saved you. Go in peace."

TOUR WITH THE TWELVE AND OTHER FOLLOWERS
Luke 8:1-3

It happened soon afterwards, that He went about through cities and villages, preaching and bringing the good news of the Kingdom of God. With Him were the twelve, and certain women who had been healed of evil spirits and infirmities: Mary who was called Magdalene, from whom seven demons had gone out; and Joanna, the wife of Chuzas, Herod's steward; Susanna; and many others; who ministered to them from their possessions.

BLASPHEMOUS ACCUSATION BY THE PHARISEES
Matthew 12:22-37; Mark 3:20-30

The multitude came together again, so that they could not so much as eat bread. When His friends heard it, they went out to seize Him: for they said, "He is insane."

Then one possessed by a demon, blind and mute, was brought to Him and He healed him, so that the blind and mute man both spoke and saw. All the multitudes were amazed, and said, "Can this be the son of David?"

The Scribes and the Pharisees came down from Jerusalem and when the Pharisees heard it, they said, "This man does not cast out demons, except by Beelzebul, the prince of the demons."

Knowing their thoughts, He summoned them and said to them, "How can Satan cast out Satan? Every kingdom divided against itself is brought to desolation, and every city or house divided against itself will not stand. If Satan casts out Satan, he is divided against himself. How then will his kingdom stand? If Satan has risen up against himself, and is divided, he can't stand, but has an end. If I by Beelzebul cast out demons, by whom do your children cast them out? Therefore they will be your judges. But if I by the Spirit of God cast out demons, then the Kingdom of God has come upon you.

"Or how can one enter into the house of the strong man, and plunder his goods, unless he first bind the strong man? Then he will plunder his house.

"He who is not with Me is against Me, and he who doesn't gather with Me, scatters. Therefore most assuredly I tell you, every sin and blasphemy will be forgiven the children of men, including their blasphemies with which they may blaspheme; but the blasphemy against the Spirit will not be forgiven men. Whoever speaks a word against the Son of Man, it will be forgiven him; but whoever speaks against the Holy Spirit, it will not be forgiven him, neither in this world, nor in that which is to come. He is guilty of an eternal sin." Jesus said this because they said, 'He has an unclean spirit.'

"Either make the tree good, and its fruit good, or make the tree corrupt, and its fruit corrupt; for the tree is known by its fruit. You offspring of vipers, how can you, being evil, speak good things? For out of the abundance of the heart, the mouth speaks. The good man out of his good treasure brings out good things, and the evil man out of his evil treasure brings out evil things. I tell you that every idle word that men speak, they will give account of it in the day of judgment. For by your words you will be justified, and by your words you will be condemned."

AN EVIL GENERATION SEEKS AFTER A SIGN
Matthew 12:38-45

Then certain of the Scribes and Pharisees answered, "Teacher, we want to see a sign from You."

But He answered them, "An evil and adulterous generation seeks after a sign, but no sign will be given it but the sign of Jonah the prophet. For as Jonah was three days and three nights in the belly of the whale, so will the Son of Man be three days and three nights in the heart of the earth. The men of Nineveh will stand up in the judgment with this generation, and will condemn it, for they repented at the preaching of Jonah; and behold, someone greater than Jonah is here. The Queen of the South will rise up in the judgment with this generation, and will condemn it, for she came from the ends of the earth to hear the wisdom of Solomon; and behold, someone greater than Solomon is here.

"But the unclean spirit, when he is gone out of the man, passes through waterless places, seeking rest, and doesn't find it. Then he says, 'I will return into my house from which I came out,' and when he has come back, he finds it empty, swept, and put in order. Then he goes, and takes with himself seven other spirits more evil than he is, and they enter in and dwell there. The last state of that man becomes worse than the first. Even so will it be also to this evil generation."

NEW SPIRITUAL TIES
Matthew 12:46-50; Mark 3:31-35; Luke 8:19-21

While He was yet speaking to the multitudes, behold, His mother and brothers came to Him, and they could not come near Him for the crowd so they stood outside, seeking to speak to Him. Then they sent to Him, calling Him. A multitude was sitting around Him, and they told Him, "Your mother and Your brothers and Your sisters stand outside, desiring to see You."

But He answered them, "Who is My mother? Who are My brothers?" Looking around at those who sat around Him, He stretched out His hand towards His disciples, and said, "Behold, My mother and My brothers! They are these who hear the word of God, and do it. For whoever does the will of My Father Who is in Heaven and whoever does the will of God, he is My brother, and sister, and mother."

THE PARABLE OF THE SOILS
Matthew 13:1-23; Mark 4:1-25; Luke 8:4-18

On that day Jesus went out of the house, and sat by the seaside and He began to teach. When a great multitude came together, and people from every city were coming to Him, He entered into a boat, and sat, and all the multitude stood on the beach and He spoke many things in parables saying, "Listen! behold, the farmer went out to sow his seed. As he sowed, some fell along the road, and it was trampled under foot, and the birds of the sky devoured it. Other seed fell on the rocky ground, where they didn't have much soil, and as soon as it grew, when the sun had risen, they were scorched and it withered away, because it had no moisture and because they had no root. Other fell amid the thorns, and the thorns grew with it, and choked it and it yielded no fruit. Other fell into the good ground, and grew, and brought forth fruit one hundred times as much, some sixty, and some thirty."

As He said these things, He called out, "He who has ears to hear, let him hear!"

When He was alone, those who were around Him with the twelve disciples came and asked Him about the parables; "Why do You speak to them in parables? What does this parable mean?"

"To you it is given to know the mysteries of the Kingdom of God, but to the rest in parables; that 'seeing they may not see, and hearing they may not understand.' For whoever has, to him will be given, and he will have abundance, but whoever doesn't have, from him will be taken away even that which he has. Therefore I speak to them in parables, because seeing they don't see, and hearing, they don't hear, neither do they understand. In them the prophecy of Isaiah is fulfilled, which says,

> 'By hearing you will hear,
>   and will in no way understand;
>   seeing you will see,
>   and will in no way perceive:
>   for this people's heart has grown callous,
>   their ears are dull of hearing,
>   they have closed their eyes; or else perhaps they might perceive with
>   their eyes, hear with their ears, understand with their heart, and should
>   turn again; and I would heal them.'

"But blessed are your eyes, for they see; and your ears, for they hear. For most assuredly I tell you that many prophets and righteous men desired to see the things which you see, and didn't see them; and to hear the things which you hear, and didn't hear them."

He said to them, "Don't you understand this parable? How will you understand all of the parables? Hear, then, the parable of the farmer. The seed is the word of God and the farmer sows the word. This is what was sown by the roadside. When anyone hears the word of the Kingdom, and doesn't understand it, then the devil comes, and takes away the word from their heart, that they may not believe and be saved. Those on the rock and on the rocky places are they who, when they hear, receive the word with joy; but these have no root, who believe for a while, but when oppression or persecution arises because of the word, immediately he stumbles and they fall away in time of temptation. That which fell among the thorns, these are those who have heard the word and as they go on their way they are choked with cares of this age, deceitfulness of riches, the lusts of other things, and pleasures of life, and bring no fruit to maturity. All these things choke the word, and he becomes unfruitful. That which was sown in the good ground, these are such as in an honest and good heart, having heard the word, understand it and accept it, hold it tightly, and bring forth fruit with patience, some one hundred times as much, some sixty, and some thirty."

He said to them, "No one, when he has lit a lamp, covers it with a container, or puts it under a bed; but puts it on a stand, that those who enter in may see the light. For nothing is hidden, that will not be revealed; nor anything secret, that will not be known and come to light. Be careful therefore how you hear. If any man has ears to hear, let him hear." He said to them, "Take heed what you hear. With whatever measure you measure, it will be measured to you, and more will be given to you who hear. For whoever has, to him more will be given; and whoever doesn't have, from him will be taken away even that which he thinks he has."

THE PARABLE OF THE SEED'S SPONTANEOUS GROWTH
Mark 4:26-29

He said, "The Kingdom of God is as if a man should cast seed on the earth, and should sleep and rise night and day, and the seed should spring up and grow, he doesn't know how. For the earth bears fruit: first the blade, then the ear, then the full grain in the ear. But when the fruit is ripe, immediately he puts forth the sickle, because the harvest has come."

THE PARABLE OF THE TARES
Matthew 13:24-30

He set another parable before them, saying, "The Kingdom of Heaven is like a man who sowed good seed in his field, but while people slept, his enemy came and sowed darnel also among the wheat, and went away. But when the blade sprang up and brought forth fruit, then the darnel appeared also.

"The servants of the householder came and said to him, 'Sir, didn't you sow good seed in your field? Where did this darnel come from?'

"He said to them, 'An enemy has done this.'

"The servants asked him, 'Do you want us to go and gather them up?'

"But he said, 'No, lest perhaps while you gather up the darnel, you root up the wheat with them. Let both grow together until the harvest, and in the harvest time I will tell the reapers, "First, gather up the darnel, and bind them in bundles to burn them; but gather the wheat into my barn."'"

THE PARABLE OF THE MUSTARD SEED
Matthew 13:31-32; Mark 4:30-32

He set another parable before them, saying, "How will we liken the Kingdom of God? Or with what parable will we illustrate it? The Kingdom of Heaven is like a grain of mustard seed, which a man took, and sowed in his field; which indeed is smaller than all seeds that are on the earth, but when it is sown, and it has grown, it is greater than the herbs, and becomes a tree and puts out great branches, so that the birds of the air come and lodge in its branches and under its shadow."

THE PARABLE OF THE LEAVENED LOAF
Matthew 13:33-35; Mark 4:33-34

He spoke another parable to them. "The Kingdom of Heaven is like yeast, which a woman took, and hid in three measures of meal, until it was all leavened."

Jesus spoke all these things in parables to the multitudes; with many such parables He spoke the word to them, as they were able to hear it. Without a parable, He didn't speak to them, that it might be fulfilled which was spoken through the prophet, saying,

> "I will open My mouth in parables;
> I will utter things hidden from the foundation of the world."

Privately to His own disciples He explained all things.

THE PARABLE OF THE TARES EXPLAINED
Matthew 13:36-43

Then Jesus sent the multitudes away, and went into the house. His disciples came to Him, saying, "Explain to us the parable of the darnel of the field."

He answered them, "He Who sows the good seed is the Son of Man, the field is the world; and the good seed, these are the children of the Kingdom; and the darnel are the children of the evil one. The enemy who sowed them is the devil. The harvest is the end of the age, and the reapers are angels.

"As therefore the darnel is gathered up and burned with fire; so will it be at the end of this age. The Son of Man will send out His angels, and they will gather out of His Kingdom all things that cause stumbling, and those who do iniquity, and will cast them into the furnace of fire. There will be weeping and the gnashing of teeth. Then the righteous will shine forth like the sun in the Kingdom of their Father. He who has ears to hear, let him hear.

THE PARABLE OF THE HIDDEN TREASURE
Matthew 13:44

"Again, the Kingdom of Heaven is like a treasure hidden in the field, which a man found, and hid. In his joy, he goes and sells all that he has, and buys that field.

THE PARABLE OF THE PEARL OF GREAT PRICE
Matthew 13:45-46

"Again, the Kingdom of Heaven is like a man who is a merchant seeking fine pearls, who having found one pearl of great price, he went and sold all that he had, and bought it.

THE PARABLE OF THE DRAGNET
Matthew 13:47-50

"Again, the Kingdom of Heaven is like a dragnet, that was cast into the sea, and gathered some fish of every kind, which, when it was filled, they drew up on the beach. They sat down, and gathered the good into containers, but the bad they threw away. So will it be in the end of the world. The angels will come forth, and separate the wicked from among the righteous, and will cast them into the furnace of fire. There will be the weeping and the gnashing of teeth."

THE PARABLE OF THE HOUSEHOLDER
Matthew 13:51-52

Jesus said to them, "Have you understood all these things?"

They answered Him, "Yes, Lord."

He said to them, "Therefore, every Scribe who has been made a disciple in the

Kingdom of Heaven is like a man who is a householder, who brings out of his treasure new and old things."

THE CALMING OF THE STORM
Matthew 13:53,8:18,23-27; Mark 4:35-41; Luke 8:22-25

It happened that when Jesus had finished these parables, He departed from there.

Now it happened on one of those days when evening had come and when Jesus saw great multitudes around Him, that He entered into a boat, Himself and His disciples, and He said to them, "Let's go over to the other side of the lake." So they launched out. Leaving the multitude, they took Him with them, even as He was, in the boat. Other small boats were also with Him. But as they sailed, He fell asleep. Behold, a great tempest arose in the sea, so much that the boat was covered with the waves. This great wind storm came down on the lake and the waves beat into the boat, and they were taking on dangerous amounts of water.

He Himself was in the stern, asleep on the cushion, and they came to Him, and awoke Him, saying, "Save us, Lord! Master, Master, we are dying! Teacher, don't You care that we are dying?"

He awoke, and rebuked the wind and said to the sea and the raging of the water, "Peace! Be still!" and the wind ceased, and it was a great calm. He said to them, "Where is your faith? Why are you fearful, oh you of little faith? How is it that you have no faith?"

Being afraid they marveled, saying one to another, "What kind of man is this and Who is this, then, that He commands even the winds and the water, and they obey Him?"

GADARENE DEMONIACS HEALED WITH OPPOSITION
Matthew 8:28-34; Mark 5:1-20; Luke 8:26-39

By boat He came to the other side of the sea at the country of the Gadarenes, which is opposite Galilee. When Jesus had come out of the boat and stepped ashore, two people possessed by demons met Him there, coming out of the tombs, exceedingly fierce, so that nobody could pass by that way. These men wore no clothes, and didn't live in a house, but in the tombs. For the unclean spirit had often seized the men, and they were kept under guard, and bound with chains and fetters. They would break the bands apart, and were driven by the demons into the desert. Nobody had the strength to tame them. Always, night and day, in the tombs and in the mountains, they were crying out, and cutting themselves with stones.

One of the men cried out when he saw Jesus from afar, he ran and fell down before Him, and with a loud voice said, "What do I have to do with You, Jesus, You Son of the Most High God? I beg You, don't torment me! Have You come here to torment us before the time? I adjure You by God, don't torment me." These both cried out the same thing over and over.

Jesus was already commanding the unclean spirit to come out of the man saying, "Come out of the man, you unclean spirit!"

Jesus then asked him, "What is your name?"

He said, "My name is Legion for we are many," for many demons had entered into him. They begged Him that He would not send them away out of the country or command them to go into the abyss.

Now there was there a great herd of many pigs feeding far away from them on the mountain, and they begged Him that He would allow them to enter into those saying, "If You cast us out, permit us to go away into the herd of pigs."

He allowed them and said to them, "Go!"

The demons came out from the men, and entered into the pigs: and behold, and the whole herd, about two thousand, rushed down the steep bank into the lake, and were drowned.

When those who fed them saw what had happened, they fled, and told everything, including what happened to those who were possessed with demons to the city and in the country. Behold, all the city came out to meet Jesus and the people went out to see what had happened. They came to Jesus, and found the men from whom the demons had gone out, sitting at Jesus' feet, clothed and in their right mind; and they were afraid. Those who saw it told them how those who had been possessed by demons were healed. All the people of the surrounding country of the Gadarenes asked and begged Him to depart from them and from their borders for they were very much afraid. He entered into the boat, and returned to Galilee.

As He was entering into the boat, one of the men from whom the demons had gone out begged Him that he might go with Him, but Jesus didn't allow him but sent him away, saying, "Return to your house, to your friends, and declare what great things the Lord God has done for you and how He had mercy on you." He went his way, proclaiming throughout the whole city and in Decapolis what great things Jesus had done for him and everyone marveled.

RETURN TO GALILEE
TOUCHING THE HEM OF THE GARMENT
RAISING OF JAIRUS' DAUGHTER
Matthew 9:18-26; Mark 5:21-43; Luke 8:40-56

It happened, when Jesus returned and had crossed back over in the boat to the other side, that the great multitude welcomed Him, for they were all waiting for Him. He was by the sea and behold, there came a man, a ruler of the synagogue, named Jairus. He came and fell down at Jesus' feet, and begged Him much to come into his house, for he had an only daughter, about twelve years of age, and she was dying. Jairus said, "My little daughter is at the point of death. Please come and lay Your hands on her, that she may be made healthy, and live."

THREE MIRACLES OF HEALING
ANOTHER BLASPHEMOUS ACCUSATION
Matthew 9:27-34

As Jesus passed by from there, two blind men followed Him, calling out and saying, "Have mercy on us, son of David!"

When He had come into the house, the blind men came to Him. Jesus said to them, "Do you believe that I am able to do this?"

They told Him, "Yes, Lord."

Then He touched their eyes, saying, "According to your faith be it done to you." Their eyes were opened. Jesus strictly charged them, saying, "See that no one knows about this." But they went out and spread abroad His fame in all that land.

As they went out, behold, a mute man who was demon possessed was brought to Him. When the demon was cast out, the mute man spoke. The multitudes marveled, saying, "Nothing like this has ever been seen in Israel!"

But the Pharisees said, "By the prince of the demons, He casts out demons."

FINAL VISIT TO NAZARETH
Matthew 13:54-58; Mark 6:1-6a

He went out from there. Coming into His own country and His disciples followed Him. When the Sabbath had come, He taught them in their synagogue, so that many were astonished, and said, "Where did this man get these things? Where did this man get this wisdom, and these mighty works come about by His hands? Isn't this the carpenter's son, a carpenter Himself? Isn't His mother called Mary, and His brothers, James, Joses, Simon, and Judas? Aren't all of His sisters with us? Where then did this man get all of these things?" They were offended by Him.

But Jesus said to them, "A prophet is not without honor, except in his own country, and among his own relatives, and in his own house."

He didn't do many mighty works there because of their unbelief except that He laid His hands on a few sick folk, and healed them. He marveled because of their unbelief.

SHEEP WITHOUT A SHEPHERD
THE PLENTIFUL HARVEST
Matthew 9:35-38; Mark 6:6b

Jesus went about all the cities and the villages, teaching in their synagogues, and preaching the gospel of the Kingdom, and healing every disease and every sickness among the people. But when He saw the multitudes, He was moved with compassion for them, because they were harassed and scattered, like sheep without a shepherd. Then He said to His disciples, "The harvest indeed is plentiful, but the laborers are few. Pray therefore that the Lord of the harvest will send out laborers into His harvest."

COMMISSIONING OF THE TWELVE
Matthew 10:1-42; Mark 6:7-11; Luke 9:1-5

He called the twelve disciples together, and gave them power and authority over all demons, to cast them out, and to cure every disease and every sickness.

Now the names of the twelve apostles are these. The first, Simon, who is called Peter; Andrew, his brother; James the son of Zebedee; John, his brother; Philip; Bartholomew; Thomas; Matthew the tax collector; James the son of Alphaeus; and Lebbaeus, whose surname was Thaddaeus; Simon the Canaanite; and Judas Iscariot, who also betrayed Him.

He sent them forth two by two to preach the Kingdom of God, and to heal the sick. He said to them and charged them, "Take nothing for your journey -- neither staffs, except a staff only, maybe one, nor wallet, nor bread, nor money; don't take any gold, nor silver, nor brass in your money belts. Wear sandals not shoes, neither have two coats apiece for the laborer is worthy of his food.

"Into whatever city or village you enter, find out who in it is worthy; and stay there until you go on. Into whatever house you enter, greet it, stay there, and depart from there. If the household is worthy, let your peace come on it, but if it isn't worthy, let your peace return to you. As many as don't receive you, nor hear your words, when you depart from that city or that house, shake off even the dust from your feet for a testimony against them. Most assuredly I tell you, it will be more tolerable for the land of Sodom and Gomorrah in the day of judgment than for that city.

"Don't go among the Gentiles, and don't enter into any city of the Samaritans. Rather, go to the lost sheep of the house of Israel. As you go, preach, saying, 'The Kingdom of Heaven is at hand!' Heal the sick, cleanse the lepers, and cast out demons. Freely you received, so freely give.

"Behold, I send you out as sheep in the midst of wolves. Therefore be wise as serpents, and harmless as doves. But beware of men: for they will deliver you up to councils, and in their synagogues they will scourge you. Yes, and you will be brought before governors and kings for My sake, for a testimony to them and to the Gentiles. But when they deliver you up, don't be anxious how or what you will say, for it will be given you in that hour what you will say. For it is not you who speak, but the Spirit of your Father Who speaks in you.

"Brother will deliver up brother to death, and the father his child. Children will rise up against parents, and cause them to be put to death. You will be hated by all men for My name's sake, but he who endures to the end will be saved. But when they persecute you in this city, flee into the next, for most assuredly I tell you, you will not have gone through the cities of Israel, until the Son of Man has come.

"A disciple is not above his teacher, nor a servant above his lord. It is enough for the disciple that he be like his teacher, and the servant like his lord. If they have called the master of the house Beelzebul, how much more those of his household! Therefore don't be afraid of them, for there is nothing covered that will not be revealed; and hidden that will not be known. What I tell you in the darkness, speak in the light; and what you hear whispered in the ear, proclaim on the housetops. Don't be afraid of those who kill the body, but are not able to kill the soul. Rather, fear Him Who is able to destroy both soul and body in Gehenna.

"Aren't two sparrows sold for an assarion? Not one of them falls on the ground apart from your Father's will, but the very hairs of your head are all numbered. Therefore don't be afraid. You are of more value than many sparrows. Everyone therefore who confesses Me before men, him I will also confess before My Father Who is in Heaven. But whoever denies Me before men, him I will also deny before My Father Who is in Heaven.

"Don't think that I came to send peace on the earth. I didn't come to send peace, but a sword. For I came to set a man at odds against his father, and a daughter against her mother, and a daughter-in-law against her mother-in-law. A man's foes will be those of his own household. He who loves father or mother more than Me is not worthy of Me; and he who loves son or daughter more than Me isn't worthy of Me. He who doesn't take his cross and follow after Me, isn't worthy of Me. He who finds his life will lose it; and he who loses his life for My sake will find it. He who receives you receives Me, and he who receives Me receives Him Who sent Me. He who receives a prophet in the name of a prophet will receive a prophet's reward: and he who receives a righteous man in the name of a righteous man will receive a righteous man's reward. Whoever gives one of these little ones just a cup of cold water to drink in the name of a disciple, most assuredly I tell you he will in no way lose his reward."

WORKERS ARE SENT FORTH
Matthew 11:1; Mark 6:12-13; Luke 9:6

They departed, and went throughout the villages, preaching the gospel, and healing everywhere. They went out and preached that people should repent. They cast out many demons, and anointed many with oil who were sick, and healed them.

It happened that when Jesus had finished directing His twelve disciples, He departed from there to teach and preach in their cities.

HEROD'S MISTAKEN IDENTIFICATION OF JESUS
Matthew 14:1-2; Mark 6:14-16; Luke 9:7-9

At that time, King Herod the tetrarch heard the report concerning Jesus for His name had become known, and of all that was done by Him; and he was very perplexed, because it was said by some that John had risen from the dead, and by some that Elijah had appeared, and by others that one of the old prophets had risen again.

Herod said to his servants, "John I beheaded, but Who is this, about Whom I hear such things? This is John the Baptist. He is risen from the dead. That is why these powers work in Him." He sought to see Him. But others said, "It is Elijah." Others said, "It is the Prophet, or like one of the prophets."

THE EARLIER IMPRISONMENT AND BEHEADING OF JOHN
Matthew 14:3-12; Mark 6:17-29

For earlier Herod had laid hold of John, and bound him, and put him in prison for the sake of Herodias, his brother Philip's wife for he had married her. For John said to him, "It is not lawful for you to have her, your brother's wife." Herodias set herself against him, and desired to kill him, but she couldn't for Herod feared John, knowing that he was a righteous and holy man, and kept him safe. When he heard him, he did many things, and he heard him gladly. Yet when he would have put him to death, he feared the multitude, because they counted him as a prophet.

But when Herod's birthday came, he made a supper for his nobles, the high officers, and the chief men of Galilee. When the daughter of Herodias danced among them and pleased Herod and those sitting with him, the king said to the young lady, "Ask me whatever you want, and I will give it to you." He swore to her, "Whatever you shall ask of me, I will give you, up to half of my kingdom" and he promised with an oath to give her whatever she should ask.

She went out, and said to her mother, "What shall I ask?"

She said, "The head of John the Baptist."

She came in immediately with haste to the king, and asked, "I want you to give me right now the head of John the Baptist on a platter."

The king was grieved and exceedingly sorry, but for the sake of his oaths, and of those who sat at the table with him, immediately the king sent out a soldier of his guard, and commanded to bring John's head and he commanded it to be given to the young lady.

His head was brought on a platter, and given to the young lady: and she brought it to her mother. When His disciples heard this, they came, and took the body, and buried it in a tomb; and they went and told Jesus.

RETURN OF THE WORKERS
Mark 6:30; Luke 9:10a

The apostles, when they had returned gathered themselves together to Jesus, and they told Him what things they had done and whatever they had taught.

WITHDRAWAL FROM GALILEE
Matthew 14:13-14; Mark 6:31-34; Luke 9:10b-11; John 6:1-3

After these things, He withdrew from there in a boat to the other side of the sea of Galilee, which is also called the Sea of Tiberias, to a deserted place near the city called Bethsaida. But the multitudes, perceiving it, followed Him on foot from the cities and they arrived before them and came together to Him. A great multitude followed Him, because they saw His signs which He did on those who were sick.

Jesus went up into the mountain, and He sat there with His disciples. He said to them, "You come apart into a deserted place, and rest awhile." For there were many coming and going, and they had no leisure so much as to eat.

Jesus went out, and He saw a great multitude. He had compassion on them because they were like sheep without a shepherd, and He began to teach them many things. He welcomed them, and spoke to them of the Kingdom of God, and He cured those who needed healing.

FEEDING THE FIVE THOUSAND
Matthew 14:15-21; Mark 6:35-44; Luke 9:12-17; John 6:4-13

Now the Passover, the feast of the Jews, was at hand.

Jesus therefore lifting up His eyes, and seeing that a great multitude was coming to Him, said to Philip, "Where are we to buy bread, that these may eat?" This He said to test him, for He Himself knew what He would do.

Philip answered Him, "Two hundred denarii worth of bread is not sufficient for them, that everyone of them may receive a little."

It was now late in the day and evening had come. The twelve disciples came to Him and said, "This place is deserted, and the hour is already late. Send the multitude away, that they may go into the surrounding villages and farms, and lodge, and get provisions, and buy themselves food for they have nothing to eat and we are here in a deserted place."

But He said to them, "They don't need to go away. You give them something to eat."

They asked Him, "Shall we go and buy two hundred denarii worth of bread, and give them something to eat?"

He said to them, "How many loaves do you have? Go see."

One of His disciples, Andrew, Simon Peter's brother, said to Him, "There is a boy here who has five barley loaves and two fish, but what are these among so many?"

When they knew for sure, they said, "We have no more than five loaves and two fish, unless we should go and buy food for all these people. There were about five thousand men besides women and children.

He said, "Bring them here to Me."

He said to His disciples, "Make them sit down on the green grass in groups of about fifty each." They did so, and made them all sit down. They sat down in ranks, by hundreds and by fifties. Now there was much grass in that place.

He took the five loaves and the two fish, and looking up to the sky and Heaven, He blessed them, and broke them, and gave them to the disciples to set before the multitude. They all ate, and were all filled. When they were filled, He said to His disciples, "Gather up the broken pieces which are left over, that nothing be lost." They gathered up twelve baskets of broken pieces and also of the fish that were left over.

AN ATTEMPT TO MAKE JESUS KING
Matthew 14:22-23; Mark 6:45-46; John 6:14-15

Immediately Jesus made the disciples get into the boat, and to go ahead of Him to the other side, to Bethsaida, while He sent the multitudes away.

When therefore the people saw the sign which Jesus did, they said, "This is truly the Prophet Who comes into the world." Jesus therefore, perceiving that they were about to come and take Him by force, to make Him king, sent the multitudes away, then He went up into the mountain by Himself to pray. When evening had come, He was there alone.

JESUS WALKS ON THE WATER
Matthew 14:24-33; Mark 6:47-52; John 6:16-21

When evening came, His disciples went down to the sea, and they entered into the boat, and were going over the sea to Capernaum. It was now dark, and Jesus had not come to them.

When therefore they had rowed the boat about twenty-five or thirty stadia, they were in the middle of the sea, distressed by the waves, for the wind was contrary. The sea was tossed by a great wind blowing.

In the fourth watch of the night, Jesus came to them, walking on the sea and He would have passed by them. They saw Jesus walking on the sea, and drawing near to the boat; and they were afraid saying, "It's a ghost!" and they cried out for fear.

But immediately Jesus spoke to them, saying "Cheer up! I AM! It is I! Don't be afraid."

Peter answered Him and said, "Lord, if it is You, command me to come to You on the waters."

He said, "Come!"

Peter stepped down from the boat, and walked on the waters to come to Jesus. But when he saw that the wind was strong, he was afraid, and beginning to sink, he cried out, saying, "Lord, save me!"

Immediately Jesus stretched out His hand, took hold of him, and said to him, "You of little faith, why did you doubt?"

They were willing therefore to receive Him into the boat. When they got up into the boat, the wind ceased. Those who were in the boat were very amazed among themselves, and marveled for they hadn't understood about the loaves, but their hearts were hardened. They came and worshiped Him, saying, "You are truly the Son of God!"

Immediately the boat was at the land where they were going.

GENNESARET HEALINGS
Matthew 14:34-36; Mark 6:53-56

When they had crossed over, they came to the land of Gennesaret and moored to the shore. When they had come out of the boat, immediately the men of that place recognized Him, they sent and ran into all that surrounding region, and brought to Him all who were sick, on their mats, to where they heard He was.

Wherever He entered, into villages, or into cities, or into the country, they laid the sick in the marketplaces, and they begged Him that they might just touch the fringe of His garment. As many as touched it were made whole.

THE TRUE BREAD OF LIFE
John 6:22-59

On the next day, the multitude that stood on the other side of the sea saw that there was no other boat there, except the one in which His disciples had embarked, and that Jesus hadn't entered with His disciples into the boat, but His disciples had gone away alone. However boats from Tiberias came near to the place where they ate the bread after the Lord had given thanks. When the multitude therefore saw that Jesus wasn't there, nor His disciples, they themselves got into the boats, and came to Capernaum, seeking Jesus.

When they found Him on the other side of the sea, they asked Him, "Rabbi, when did You come here?"

Jesus answered them, "Most assuredly I tell you, you seek Me, not because you saw signs, but because you ate of the loaves, and were filled. Don't work for the food which perishes, but for the food which remains to eternal life, which the Son of Man will give to you. For God the Father has sealed Him."

They said therefore to Him, "What must we do, that we may work the works of God?"

Jesus answered them, "This is the work of God, that you believe in Him Whom He has sent."

They said therefore to Him, "What then do You do for a sign, that we may see, and believe You? What work do You do? Our fathers ate the manna in the wilderness. As it is written,

> 'He gave them bread out of Heaven to eat.'"

Jesus therefore said to them, "Most assuredly, I tell you, it wasn't Moses who gave you the bread out of Heaven, but My Father gives you the true bread out of Heaven. For the bread of God is that which comes down out of Heaven, and gives life to the world."

They said therefore to Him, "Lord, always give us this bread."

Jesus said to them. "I am the bread of life. He who comes to Me will not be hungry, and he who believes in Me will never be thirsty. But I told you that you have seen Me, and yet you don't believe. All those who the Father gives Me will come to Me. Him who comes to Me I will in no way cast out. For I have come down from Heaven, not to do My Own will, but the will of Him Who sent Me. This is the will of My Father Who sent Me, that of all He has given to Me I should lose nothing, but should raise him up at the last day. This is the will of the One Who sent Me, that everyone who sees the Son, and believes in Him, should have eternal life; and I will raise him up at the last day."

The Jews therefore murmured concerning Him, because He said, "I am the bread which came down out of Heaven." They said, "Isn't this Jesus, the son of Joseph, Whose father and mother we know? How then does He say, 'I have come down out of Heaven?'"

Therefore Jesus answered them, "Don't murmur among yourselves. No one can come to Me unless the Father Who sent Me draws him, and I will raise him up in the last day. It is written in the prophets,

> 'They will all be taught by God.'

"Therefore everyone who hears from the Father, and has learned, comes to Me. Not that anyone has seen the Father, except He who is from God. He has seen the Father. Most assuredly, I tell you, he who believes in Me has eternal life. I am the bread of life. Your fathers ate the manna in the wilderness, and they died. This is the bread which comes down out of Heaven, that anyone may eat of it and not die. I am the living bread which came down out of Heaven. If anyone eats of this bread, he will live forever. Yes, the bread which I will give for the life of the world is My flesh."

The Jews therefore contended with one another, saying, "How can this man give us His flesh to eat?"

Jesus therefore said to them, "Most assuredly I tell you, unless you eat the flesh of the Son of Man and drink His blood, you don't have life in yourselves. He who eats My flesh and drinks My blood has eternal life, and I will raise him up at the last day. For My flesh is food indeed, and My blood is drink indeed. He who eats My flesh and drinks My blood lives in Me, and I in him. As the living Father sent Me, and I live because of the Father; so he who feeds on Me, he will also live because of Me. This is the bread which came down out of Heaven -- not as our fathers ate the manna, and died. He who eats this bread will live forever." These things He said in the synagogue, as He taught in Capernaum.

DEFECTION OF SOME DISCIPLES
John 6:60-71

Therefore many of His disciples, when they heard this, said, "This is a hard saying! Who can listen to it?"

But Jesus knowing in Himself that His disciples murmured at this, said to them, "Does this cause you to stumble? Then what if you would see the Son of Man ascending to where He was before? It is the Spirit Who gives life. The flesh profits nothing. The words that I speak to you are spirit, and are life. But there are some of you who don't believe." For Jesus knew from the beginning who they were who didn't believe, and who it was who would betray Him. He said, "For this cause have I said to you that no one can come to Me, unless it is given to him by My Father."

At this, many of His disciples went back, and walked no more with Him.

Jesus said therefore to the twelve, "You don't also want to go away, do you?"

Simon Peter answered Him, "Lord, to whom would we go? You have the words of eternal life. We have come to believe and know that You are the Christ, the Son of the living God."

Jesus answered them, "Didn't I choose you, the twelve, and one of you is a devil?" Now He spoke of Judas, the son of Simon Iscariot, for it was he who would betray Him, being one of the twelve.

THE TRADITIONS OF MEN
Matthew 15:1-20; Mark 7:1-23; John 7:1

After these things, Jesus was walking in Galilee, for He wouldn't walk in Judea, because the Jews sought to kill Him.

Then Pharisees and some of the Scribes came to Jesus from Jerusalem, and when they saw some of His disciples eating bread with defiled, that is, unwashed, hands, they found fault. (For the Pharisees, and all the Jews, don't eat unless they wash their hands and forearms, holding to the tradition of the Elders. They don't eat when they come from the marketplace, unless they bathe themselves, and there are many other things, which they have received to hold to: washings of cups, pitchers, bronze vessels, and couches.) They asked Jesus, "Why do Your disciples not walk according to but disobey the tradition of the Elders? For they don't wash their hands when they eat bread."

He answered them, "Why do you also disobey the commandment of God because of your tradition? For God commanded and Moses said, 'Honor your father and your mother,' and, 'He who speaks evil of father or mother, let him be put to death.' But you say, 'Whoever may tell his father or his mother, "Whatever help you might otherwise have gotten from me is a gift devoted to God, that it is Corban, that is to say, given to God;" he shall not honor his father or mother.' Then you no longer allow him to do anything for his father or his mother, and by doing so you have made the commandment of God void because of your tradition which you have handed down. For you set aside the commandment of God, and hold tightly to the tradition of men -- the washing of pitchers and cups, and you do many other such things."

He said to them, "Full well do you reject the commandment of God, that you may keep your tradition. You do many things like this. You hypocrites! Well did Isaiah prophesy of you as it is written, saying,

> 'These people draw near to Me with their mouth,
>   and honor Me with their lips;
>   but their heart is far from Me.
> And in vain do they worship Me,
>   teaching as doctrine rules made by men
>   and the commandments of men.'"

He summoned the multitude, and said to them, "Hear, all of you, and understand. That which enters into the mouth doesn't defile the man; but that which proceeds out of the mouth, this defiles the man. If anyone has ears to hear, let him hear!"

Then the disciples came, and said to Him, "Do You know that the Pharisees were offended, when they heard this saying?"

But He answered, "Every plant which My Heavenly Father didn't plant will be uprooted. Leave them alone. They are blind guides of the blind. If the blind guide the blind, both will fall into a pit."

When He had entered into a house away from the multitude, Peter asked Him, "Explain the parable to us." The other disciples also asked Him about the parable.

So Jesus said, "Do you also still not understand? Don't you understand that whatever goes into the mouth passes into the belly, and then out of the body and can't defile him, because it doesn't go into his heart, but into his stomach, then into the latrine, thus making all foods clean? But the things which proceed out of the mouth come out of the heart, and they defile the man. For out of the heart come forth evil thoughts, murders, adulteries, sexual sins, thefts, false testimony, covetings, wickedness, deceit, lustful desires, an evil eye, pride, foolishness, and blasphemies. These are the evil things which come from within, and defile the man; but to eat with unwashed hands doesn't defile the man."

GENTILE WOMAN IN TYRE AND SIDON
Matthew 15:21-28; Mark 7:24-30

Jesus went out from there, and withdrew into borders of the region of Tyre and Sidon. He entered into a house, and didn't want anyone to know it, but He couldn't escape notice. Behold, a Canaanite woman whose little daughter had an unclean spirit, came out from those borders having heard of Him, came and fell down at His feet and cried, saying, "Have mercy on me, Lord, You son of David! My daughter is severely demonized!" Now the woman was a Greek, a Syrophoe-nician by race.

But He answered her not a word. His disciples came and begged Him, saying, "Send her away; for she cries after us."

But He answered, "I wasn't sent to anyone but the lost sheep of the house of Israel."

But she came and worshiped Him, saying, "Lord, help me."

But He answered, "Let the children be filled first, it is not appropriate to take the children's bread and throw it to the dogs."

But she said, "Yes, Lord, but even the dogs under the table eat the crumbs which fall from their masters' table."

Then Jesus answered her, "Woman, great is your faith! For this saying, go your way. The demon has gone out of your daughter. Be it done to you even as you desire." And her daughter was healed from that hour.

She went away to her house, and found the child having been laid on the bed, with the demon gone out.

HEALINGS IN DECAPOLIS
Matthew 15:29-31; Mark 7:31-37

Jesus departed there from the borders of Tyre and Sidon, and came near to the sea of Galilee; through the midst of the region of Decapolis.

They brought to Him one who was deaf and had an impediment in his speech. They begged Him to lay His hand on him. He took him aside from the multitude, privately, and put His fingers into his ears, and He spat, and touched his tongue. Looking up to heaven, He sighed, and said to him, "Ephphatha!" that is, "Be opened!" Immediately his ears were opened, and the impediment of his tongue was released, and he spoke clearly. He commanded them that they should tell no one, but the more He commanded them, so much the more widely they proclaimed it. They were astonished beyond measure, saying, "He has done all things well. He makes even the deaf hear, and the mute speak!"

Then Jesus went up into the mountain, and sat there. Great multitudes came to Him, having with them the lame, blind, mute, maimed, and many others, and they put them down at His feet. He healed them, so that the multitude wondered when they saw the mute speaking, injured whole, lame walking, and blind seeing -- and they glorified the God of Israel.

THE FEEDING OF THE FOUR THOUSAND
Matthew 15:32-38; Mark 8:1-9

In those days, when there was a very great multitude, and they had nothing to eat, Jesus summoned His disciples to Himself, and said, "I have compassion on the multitude, because they continue with Me now three days and have nothing to eat. I don't want to send them away to their homes fasting, or they might faint on the way for some of them have come a long way."

The disciples said to Him, "Where should we get so many loaves in a deserted place as to satisfy so great a multitude?"

Jesus said to them, "How many loaves do you have?"

They said, "Seven, and a few small fish."

He commanded the multitude to sit down on the ground; and He took the seven loaves and the fish. He gave thanks and broke them, and gave to the disciples to serve, and the disciples served the multitudes. They all ate, and were filled. They took up seven baskets full of the broken pieces that were left over. Those who ate were four thousand men, besides women and children. Then He sent them away.

ANOTHER ENCOUNTER WITH THE SADDUCEES AND PHARISEES
Matthew 15:39 - 16:4; Mark 8:10-12

Then He sent away the multitudes, got into the boat with His disciples, and came into the borders of Magdala and into the region of Dalmanutha. The Pharisees and Sadducees came out, and began to question Him. They asked Him, testing Him, to show them a sign from Heaven.

He sighed deeply in His Spirit, and said, "When it is evening, you say, 'It will be fair weather, for the sky is red.' In the morning, 'It will be foul weather today, for the sky is red and threatening.' Hypocrites! You know how to discern the appearance of the sky, but you can't discern the signs of the times! Why does this evil and adulterous generation seek after a sign? Most assuredly I tell you, there will be no sign given to it, except the sign of the prophet Jonah." He left them, and departed.

WARNINGS ABOUT THE PHARISEES, SADDUCEES, AND HERODIANS
Matthew 16:5-12; Mark 8:13-21

He left them, and again entering into the boat, departed to the other side. The disciples came to the other side and had forgotten to take bread and they didn't have more than one loaf in the boat with them. Jesus said to them and charged them, "Take heed and beware of the yeast of the Pharisees and Sadducees and the yeast of Herod."

They reasoned among themselves, saying, "It's because we brought no bread."

Jesus, perceiving it, said to them, "Having eyes, don't you see? Having ears, don't you hear? Don't you remember? Is your heart still hardened? Why do you reason among yourselves, you of little faith, 'because you have brought no bread?' Don't you yet perceive or understand, neither remember the five loaves for the five thousand, and how many baskets did you take up?

They told Him, "Twelve."

Jesus then asked them, "Nor the seven loaves for the four thousand, and how many baskets did you take up?"

They told Him, "Seven."

"How is it that you don't perceive that I didn't speak to you concerning bread? But beware of the yeast of the Pharisees and Sadducees."

Then they understood that He didn't tell them to beware of the yeast of bread, but of the teaching of the Pharisees and Sadducees.

HEALING OF A BLIND MAN AT BETHSAIDA
Mark 8:22-26

He came to Bethsaida. They brought a blind man to Him, and begged Him to touch him. He took hold of the blind man by the hand, and brought him out of the village. When He had spit on his eyes, and laid His hands on him, He asked him if he saw anything.

He looked up, and said, "I see men; for I see them like trees walking."

Then again He laid His hands on his eyes. He looked intently, and was restored, and saw everyone clearly. He sent him away to his house, saying, "Don't enter into the village, nor tell anyone in the village."

PETER'S CONFESSION OF CHRIST
FIRST PROPHECY OF THE CHURCH
Matthew 16:13-20; Mark 8:27-30; Luke 9:18-21

Now when Jesus came into the parts and the villages of Caesarea Philippi, on the way it happened, as He was praying alone, that the disciples were with Him, and He asked them, "Who do the multitudes say that I, the Son of Man, am?"

They answered, "'John the Baptist,' but others say, 'Elijah,' and others, 'Jeremiah,' or 'one of the prophets.' They say that one of the old prophets is risen again."

He said to them, "But who do you say that I am?"

Simon Peter answered, "You are the Christ of God, the Son of the living God."

Jesus answered him, "Blessed are you, Simon Bar Jonah, for flesh and blood has not revealed this to you, but My Father Who is in Heaven. I also tell you that you are Peter, and on this rock I will build My church, and the gates of Hades will not prevail against it. I will give to you the keys of the Kingdom of Heaven, and whatever you bind on earth will be bound in Heaven; and whatever you loose on earth will be loosed in Heaven."

But then He warned and charged them, and commanded them to tell this to no one, that He is Jesus the Christ.

FIRST PREDICTION OF THE CRUCIFIXION AND RESURRECTION
Matthew 16:21-26; Mark 8:31-37; Luke 9:22-25

From that time, Jesus began to show His disciples that He, the Son of Man, must go to Jerusalem and suffer many things and be rejected by the Elders, Chief Priests , and Scribes, and be killed, and the third day be raised up. He said to His disciples, "The Son of Man must suffer many things, and be rejected by the Elders, Chief Priests , and Scribes, and be killed, and the third day be raised up."

Peter took Him aside, and began to rebuke Him, saying, "Far be it from You, Lord! This will never be done to You."

But He turned, and said to Peter, "Get behind Me, Satan! You are a stumbling -block to Me, for you are not setting your mind on the things of God, but on the things of men."

He called the multitude to Himself with His disciples, and said to them, "If anyone desires to come after Me, let him deny himself, take up his cross daily, and follow Me. For whoever desires to save his life will lose it, but whoever will lose his life for My sake and the gospel's, the same will save it and find it. For what does it profit a man if he gains the whole world, and loses or forfeits his own self and his life? Or what will a man give in exchange for his life?

THE COMING OF THE SON OF MAN AND JUDGMENT
Matthew 16:27-28; Mark 8:38-9:1; Luke 9:26-27

Then Jesus said, "For the Son of Man will come in the glory of His Father with His angels, and then He will render to everyone according to his deeds. For whoever will be ashamed of Me and of My words in this adulterous and sinful generation, of him will the Son of Man be ashamed, when He comes in His glory, and the glory of the Father, and of the holy angels. But I tell you the truth: There are some of those who stand here, who will in no way taste of death, until they see the Son of Man coming in the Kingdom of God with power."

THE TRANSFIGURATION OF JESUS
Matthew 17:1-9; Mark 9:2-10; Luke 9:28-36

It happened about eight days* after these sayings, that He took with Him Peter, John, and James, and went up onto the mountain to pray privately by them-

---

* Matthew and Mark report "Six Days" excluding the day Jesus spoke of the Kingdom and the day of the transfiguration itself.

selves. As He was praying, He was changed into another form in front of them. The appearance of His face was altered and shone like the sun, and His clothing became glistening, exceedingly white like snow, such as no launderer on earth can whiten them. They were dazzling as white as the light as He was transfigured before them. Behold, two men were talking with Him, who were Moses and Elijah, who appeared also with Him in glory, and spoke of His departure, which He was about to accomplish at Jerusalem. Now Peter and those who were with him were heavy with sleep, but when they were fully awake, they saw His glory, and the two men who stood with Him. It happened, as they were parting from Him, that Peter said to Jesus, "Master, Lord, Rabbi, it is good for us to be here. If You want, let's make three tents: one for You, and one for Moses, and one for Elijah," not knowing what he said. For he didn't know what to say, for they were very afraid.

While he said these things, a bright cloud came and overshadowed them, and they were afraid as they entered into the cloud. A voice came out of the cloud, saying, "This is My beloved Son, in Whom I am well pleased. Listen to Him!" When the disciples heard it, they fell on their faces, and were very afraid. Jesus came and touched them and said, "Get up, and don't be afraid." Lifting up their eyes, they saw no one, except Jesus alone.

As they were coming down from the mountain, Jesus commanded and charged them, saying, "Don't tell anyone what you saw, until the Son of Man has risen from the dead." They were silent, and told no one in those days any of the things which they had seen. They kept this saying to themselves, questioning what the 'rising from the dead' meant.

ELIJAH AND JOHN THE BAPTIST
THE COMING OF THE SON OF MAN
Matthew 17:10-13; Mark 9:11-13

His disciples asked Him, saying, "Then why do the Scribes say that Elijah must come first?"

Jesus answered them, "Elijah indeed comes first, and will restore all things, but I tell you that Elijah has come already, and they didn't recognize him, but did to him whatever they wanted to even as it is written about him. Even so as it is written about the Son of Man, He will also suffer many things and be despised by them."

Then the disciples understood that He spoke to them of John the Baptist.

FAITHLESSNESS AND THE HEALING OF A DEMONIC BOY
Matthew 17:14-20; Mark 9:14-29; Luke 9:37-43a

It happened on the next day, when they had come down from the mountain and were coming to the other disciples, He saw a great multitude around them, and the Scribes questioning them. Immediately all the multitude, when they saw Him, were greatly amazed, and running to Him, greeted Him.

He asked the Scribes, "What are you asking them?"

One of the multitude met Him and answered, kneeling down to Him, saying, "Teacher, Lord, I beg You to look at my son and have mercy on him, for he is my only child. He is epileptic and has a mute spirit, and suffers grievously; for he often falls into the fire, and often into the water. Behold, a spirit takes him, he suddenly cries out, and it convulses him so that he foams at the mouth, and grinds his teeth, and wastes away, and it hardly departs from him, bruising him severely. So I brought him to Your disciples, and I begged Your disciples to cast it out, and they couldn't cure him."

Jesus answered, "Faithless and perverse generation, how long shall I be with you and bear with you? Bring your son here to Me."

While he was still coming, the demon threw him down and convulsed him violently and he fell on the ground, wallowing and foaming at the mouth.

He asked his father, "How long has it been since this has come to him?"

He said, "From childhood. Often it has cast him both into the fire and into the water, to destroy him. But if You can do anything, have compassion on us, and help us."

Jesus said to him, "If you can believe, all things are possible to him who believes."

Immediately the father of the child cried out with tears, "I believe. Help my unbelief!"

When Jesus saw that a multitude came running together, He rebuked the unclean spirit saying to him, "You mute and deaf spirit, I command you, come out of him, and never enter him again!"

Having cried out, and convulsed greatly, the demon went out of him. The boy became like one dead; so much that most of them said, "He is dead." But Jesus took him by the hand, and raised him up; and he arose. Jesus then gave him back to his father and the boy was healed from that hour. They were all astonished at the majesty of God.

Then, when He had come into the house, the disciples came to Jesus privately, and said, "Why weren't we able to cast it out?"

He said to them, "Because of your unbelief. For most assuredly I tell you, if you have faith as a grain of mustard seed, you will tell this mountain, 'Move from here to there,' and it will move; and nothing will be impossible for you. Yet this kind can come out by nothing, except by prayer and fasting."

SECOND PREDICTION OF THE RESURRECTION
Matthew 17:22-23; Mark 9:30-32; Luke 9:43b-45

But while all were marveling at all the things which Jesus did, they went out from there, and passed through Galilee. He didn't want anyone to know it, for He was teaching His disciples, and He said to them, "Let these words sink into your ears, for the Son of Man will be delivered up into the hands of men and they will kill Him, and when He is killed, the third day He will be raised up." But they didn't understand this saying. It was concealed from them, that they should not perceive it, and they were afraid to ask Him about this saying. Yet they were exceedingly sorry.

PAYING THE TEMPLE TAX
Matthew 17:24-27

When they had come to Capernaum, those who collected the didrachma coins came to Peter, and said, "Doesn't your teacher pay the didrachma?"

He said, "Yes."

When he came into the house, Jesus anticipated him, saying, "What do you think, Simon? From whom do the kings of the earth receive toll or tribute? From their children, or from strangers?"

Peter said to Him, "From strangers."

Jesus said to him, "Therefore the children are exempt. But, lest we cause them to stumble, go to the sea, and cast a hook, and take up the first fish that comes up. When you have opened its mouth, you will find a stater coin. Take that, and give it to them for Me and you."

ARGUMENTS OVER GREATNESS
Matthew 18:1-5; Mark 9:33-37; Luke 9:46-48

As they were on their way to Capernaum, there arose an argument among the disciples about which of them was the greatest. When they came to Capernaum, and when He was in the house He asked them, "What were you arguing among yourselves on the way?" But they were silent.

In that hour the disciples finally came to Him, saying, "Who then is greatest in the Kingdom of Heaven?"

Jesus, perceiving the reasoning of their hearts, sat down, and said to them, "If any man wants to be first, he shall be last of all, and servant of all."

He then took a little child, and set him by His side, and taking him in His arms, He said to them, "Most assuredly I tell you, unless you turn, and become as little children, you will in no way enter into the Kingdom of Heaven. Whoever therefore humbles himself as this little child, the same is the greatest in the Kingdom of Heaven. Whoever receives this little child in My name receives Me. Whoever receives Me receives Him Who sent Me. For whoever is least among you all, this one will be great.

WARNINGS AGAINST CAUSING OTHERS TO STUMBLE
Matthew 18:6-14; Mark 9:38-50; Luke 9:49-50

"Woe to the world because of occasions of stumbling! For it must be that the offences come, but woe to that person through whom the offence comes!

John answered, "Master, Teacher, we saw someone who doesn't follow us casting out demons in Your name, and we forbade him, because he doesn't follow with us."

Jesus said to him, "Don't forbid him, for there is no one who will do a mighty work in My name, and be able quickly to speak evil of Me. For he who is not against us is for us and on our side.

"For whoever will give you a cup of water to drink in My name, because you are Christ's, most assuredly I tell you, he will in no way lose his reward. But whoever causes one of these little ones who believe in Me to stumble, it would be better for him that a huge millstone should be hung around his neck, and that he should be sunk in the depths of the sea.

"If your hand or your foot causes you to stumble, cut it off, and cast it from you. It is better for you to enter into life maimed or crippled, rather than having two hands or two feet to be cast into the eternal fire of Gehenna, the unquenchable fire, 'where their worm doesn't die, and the fire is not quenched.'

"If your eye causes you to stumble, pluck it out, and cast it from you. It is better for you to enter into life with one eye, rather than having two eyes to be cast into the Gehenna of fire, 'where their worm doesn't die, and the fire is not quenched.'

"For everyone will be salted with fire, and every sacrifice will be seasoned with salt. Salt is good, but if the salt has lost its saltiness, with what will you season it? Have salt in yourselves, and be at peace with one another.

"For the Son of Man came to save that which was lost.

"See that you don't despise one of these little ones, for I tell you that in Heaven their angels always see the face of My Father Who is in Heaven.

"What do you think? If a man has one hundred sheep, and one of them goes astray, doesn't he leave the ninety-nine, go to the mountains, and seek that which has gone astray? If he finds it, most assuredly I tell you, he rejoices over it more than over the ninety-nine which have not gone astray. Even so it is not the will of your Father Who is in Heaven that one of these little ones should perish.

FORGIVENESS OF A SINNING BROTHER
Matthew 18:15-35

"If your brother sins against you, go, show him his fault between you and him alone. If he listens to you, you have gained back your brother. But if he doesn't listen, take one or two more with you, that at the mouth of two or three witnesses every word may be established. If he refuses to listen to them, tell it to the assembly. If he refuses to hear the assembly also, let him be to you as a Gentile or a tax collector.

"Most assuredly I tell you, whatever things you will bind on earth will be bound in Heaven, and whatever things you will release on earth will be released in Heaven.

"Again, assuredly I tell you, that if two of you will agree on earth concerning anything that they will ask, it will be done for them by My Father Who is in Heaven. For where two or three are gathered together in My name, there I am in the midst of them."

Then Peter came and said to Him, "Lord, how often shall my brother sin against me, and I forgive him? Until seven times?"

Jesus said to him, "I don't tell you until seven times, but, until seventy times seven.

"Therefore the Kingdom of Heaven is like a certain king, who wanted to reconcile accounts with his servants. When he had begun to reconcile, one was brought to him who owed him ten thousand talents. But because he couldn't pay, his lord commanded him to be sold, with his wife, his children, and all that he had, and payment to be made.

"The servant therefore fell down and kneeled before him, saying, 'Lord, have patience with me, and I will repay you all!' The lord of that servant, being moved with compassion, released him, and forgave him the debt.

"But that servant went out, and found one of his fellow servants, who owed him one hundred denarii, and he grabbed him, and took him by the throat, saying, 'Pay me what you owe!'

"So his fellow servant fell down at his feet and begged him, saying, 'Have patience with me, and I will repay you!'

"He would not, but went and cast him into prison, until he should pay back that which was due. So when his fellow servants saw what was done, they were exceedingly sorry, and came and told to their lord all that was done.

"Then his lord called him in, and said to him, 'You wicked servant! I forgave you all that debt, because you begged me. Shouldn't you also have had mercy on your fellow servant, even as I had mercy on you?' His lord was angry, and delivered him to the tormentors, until he should pay all that was due to him.

"So My Heavenly Father will also do to you, if you don't each forgive your brother from your hearts for his misdeeds."

RIDICULE BY JESUS' HALF-BROTHERS
John 7:2-9

Now the feast of the Jews, the Feast of Booths, was at hand. His brothers therefore said to Him, "Depart from here, and go into Judea, that Your disciples also may see Your works which You do. For no one does anything in secret, and himself seeks to be known openly. If You do these things, reveal Yourself to the world." For even His brothers didn't believe in Him.

Jesus therefore said to them, "My time has not yet come, but your time is always ready. The world can't hate you, but it hates Me, because I testify about it, that its works are evil. You go up to the feast. I am not yet going up to this feast, because My time is not yet fulfilled." Having said these things to them, He stayed in Galilee.

JOURNEY THROUGH SAMARIA
Luke 9:51-56; John 7:10

But when His brothers had gone up to the feast, then He also went up, not publicly, but as it were in secret.

It came to pass, when the days were near that He should be taken up, He intently set His face to go to Jerusalem, and sent messengers before His face. They went, and entered into a village of the Samaritans, so as to prepare for Him. They didn't receive Him, because He was traveling with His face set towards Jerusalem. When His disciples, James and John, saw this, they said, "Lord, do You want us to command fire to come down from heaven, and destroy them, just as Elijah did?" But He turned and rebuked them, "You don't know of what kind of spirit you are. For the Son of Man didn't come to destroy men's lives, but to save them." They went to another village.

COMPLETE COMMITMENT DEMANDED
Matthew 8:19-22; Luke 9:57-62

As they went on the way, a certain man, a Scribe, came, and said to Him, "Teacher, I want to and I will follow You wherever You go, Lord."

Jesus said to him, "The foxes have holes, and the birds of the sky have nests, but the Son of Man has no place to lay His head."

He said to another of His disciples, "Follow Me!"

But he said, "Lord, allow me first to go and bury my father."

But Jesus said to him, "Follow Me, leave the dead to bury their own dead, but you go and announce the Kingdom of God."

Another also said, "I want to follow You, Lord, but first allow me to bid farewell to those who are at my house."

But Jesus said to him, "No one, having put his hand to the plow, and looking back, is fit for the Kingdom of God."

MIXED REACTION TO JESUS' TEACHING AND MIRACLES
A FRUSTRATED ATTEMPT TO ARREST JESUS
THE ADULTERESS WOMAN IS FORGIVEN
THE LIGHT OF THE WORLD
INVITATION TO BELIEVE
ATTEMPTED STONING
John 7:11-8:59

The Jews therefore sought Him at the feast, and said, "Where is He?"

There was much murmuring among the multitudes concerning Him. Some said, "He is a good man."

Others said, "Not so, but He leads the multitude astray." Yet no one spoke openly of Him for fear of the Jews.

But when it was now the midst of the feast, Jesus went up into the temple and taught. The Jews therefore marveled, saying, "How does this man know letters, having never been educated?"

Jesus therefore answered them, "My teaching is not Mine, but His Who sent Me. If anyone desires to do His will, he will know about the teaching, whether it is from God, or if I am speaking from Myself. He who speaks from himself seeks his own glory, but He Who seeks the glory of Him Who sent Him, the same is true, and there is no unrighteousness is in Him. Didn't Moses give you the law, and yet none of you keeps the law? Why do you seek to kill Me?"

The multitude answered, "You have a demon! Who seeks to kill You?"

Jesus answered them, "I did one work, and you all marvel because of it. Moses has given you circumcision (not that it is of Moses, but of the fathers), and on the Sabbath you circumcise a boy. If a boy receives circumcision on the Sabbath, that the law of Moses may not be broken, are you angry with Me, because I made a man every bit whole on the Sabbath? Don't judge according to appearance, but judge righteous judgment."

Therefore some of them of Jerusalem said, "Isn't this He Whom they seek to kill? Behold, He speaks openly, and they say nothing to Him. Can it be that the rulers indeed know that this is truly the Christ? However we know where this man comes from, but when the Christ comes, no one will know where He comes from."

Jesus therefore cried out in the temple, teaching and saying, "You both know Me, and know where I am from. I have not come of Myself, but He Who sent Me is true, Whom you don't know. I know Him, because I am from Him, and He sent Me."

They sought therefore to take Him; but no one laid a hand on Him, because

His hour had not yet come. But of the multitude, many believed in Him. They said, "When the Christ comes, He won't do more signs than those which this man has done, will He?"

The Pharisees heard the multitude murmuring these things concerning Him, and the Chief Priests and the Pharisees sent officers to arrest Him.

Then Jesus said, "I will be with you a little while longer, then I go to Him Who sent Me. You will seek Me, and won't find Me; and where I am, you can't come."

The Jews therefore said among themselves, "Where will this man go that we won't find Him? Will He go to the dispersion among the Greeks, and teach the Greeks? What is this word that He said, 'You will seek Me, and won't find Me; and where I am, you can't come?'"

Now on the last and greatest day of the feast, Jesus stood and cried out, "If anyone is thirsty, let him come to Me and drink! He who believes in Me, as the Scripture has said, from within him will flow rivers of living water." But He said this about the Spirit, which those believing in Him were to receive. For the Holy Spirit was not yet given, because Jesus wasn't yet glorified.

Many of the multitude therefore, when they heard these words, said, "This is truly the prophet."

Others said, "This is the Christ."

But some said, "What, does the Christ come out of Galilee? Hasn't the Scripture said that the Christ comes of the seed of David, and from Bethlehem, the village where David was?" So there arose a division in the multitude because of Him. Some of them would have arrested Him, but no one laid hands on Him.

The officers therefore came to the Chief Priests and Pharisees, and they said to them, "Why didn't you bring Him?"

The officers answered, "No man ever spoke like this man!"

The Pharisees therefore answered them, "You aren't also led astray, are you? Have any of the rulers believed in Him, or of the Pharisees? But this multitude that doesn't know the law is accursed."

Nicodemus (he who came to Him by night, being one of them) said to them, "Does our law judge a man, unless it first hears from him personally and knows what he does?"

They answered him, "Are you also from Galilee? Search, and see that no prophet has arisen out of Galilee."

Everyone went to his own house, but Jesus went to the Mount of Olives.

Now very early in the morning, He came again into the temple, and all the people came to Him. He sat down, and taught them. The Scribes and the Pharisees brought a woman taken in adultery. Having set her in the midst, they told Him, "Teacher, we found this woman in adultery, in the very act. Now in our law, Moses commanded us to stone such. What then do You say about her?" They said this testing Him, that they might have something to accuse Him of.

But Jesus stooped down, and wrote on the ground with His finger. But when they continued asking Him, He looked up and said to them, "He who is without sin among you, let him throw the first stone at her." Again He stooped down, and with His finger wrote on the ground.

They, when they heard it, being convicted by their conscience, went out one by one, beginning from the oldest, even to the last. Jesus was left alone with the woman where she was, in the middle. Jesus, standing up, saw her and said, "Woman, where are your accusers? Did no one condemn you?"

She said, "No one, Lord."

Jesus said, "Neither do I condemn you. Go your way. From now on, sin no more."

Again, therefore, Jesus spoke to them, saying, "I am the light of the world. He who follows Me will not walk in the darkness, but will have the light of life."

The Pharisees therefore said to Him, "You testify about Yourself. Your testimony is not valid."

Jesus answered them, "Even if I testify about Myself, My testimony is true, for I know where I came from, and where I am going; but you don't know where I came from, or where I am going. You judge according to the flesh. I judge no one. Even if I do judge, My judgment is true, for I am not alone, but I am with the Father Who sent Me. It's also written in your law that the testimony of two people is valid. I am One Who testifies about Myself, and the Father Who sent Me testifies about Me."

They said therefore to Him, "Where is Your Father?"

Jesus answered, "You know neither Me, nor My Father. If you knew Me, you would know My Father also." Jesus spoke these words in the treasury, as He taught in the temple. Yet no one arrested Him, because His hour had not yet come.

Jesus said therefore again to them, "I am going away, and you will seek Me, and you will die in your sins. Where I go, you can't come."

The Jews therefore said, "Will He kill Himself, that He says, 'Where I am going, you can't come?'"

He said to them, "You are from beneath. I am from above. You are of this world. I am not of this world. I said therefore to you that you will die in your sins; for unless you believe that I am He, you will die in your sins."

They said therefore to Him, "Who are You?"

Jesus said to them, "Just what I have been saying to you from the beginning. I have many things to speak and to judge concerning you. However He Who sent Me is true; and the things which I heard from Him, these I say to the world."

They didn't understand that He spoke to them about the Father. Jesus therefore said to them, "When you have lifted up the Son of Man, then you will know that I am He, and I do nothing of Myself, but as My Father taught Me, I say these things. He Who sent Me is with Me. The Father hasn't left Me alone, for I always do the things that are pleasing to Him." As He spoke these things, many believed in Him.

Jesus therefore said to those Jews who had believed Him, "If you remain in My word, then you are truly My disciples. You will know the truth, and the truth will make you free."

They answered Him, "We are Abraham's seed, and have never been in bondage to anyone. How do You say, 'You will be made free?'"

Jesus answered them, "Most assuredly I tell you, everyone who commits sin is the bondservant of sin. A bondservant doesn't live in the house forever. A son remains forever. If therefore the Son makes you free, you will be free indeed. I know that you are Abraham's seed, yet you seek to kill Me, because My word finds no place in you. I say the things which I have seen with My Father; and you also do the things which you have seen with your father."

They answered Him, "Our father is Abraham."

Jesus said to them, "If you were Abraham's children, you would do the works of Abraham. But now you seek to kill Me, a Man Who has told you the truth, which I heard from God. Abraham didn't do this. You do the works of your father."

They said to Him, "We were not born of sexual immorality. We have one Father, God."

Therefore Jesus said to them, "If God were your Father, you would love Me, for I came out and have come from God. For I haven't come of Myself, but He sent Me. Why don't you understand My speech? Because you can't hear My word. You are of your father, the devil, and you want to do the desires of your father. He was a murderer from the beginning, and doesn't stand in the truth, because there is no truth in him. When he speaks a lie, he speaks on his own; for he is a liar, and the father of it. But because I tell the truth, you don't believe Me. Which of you convicts Me of sin? If I tell the truth, why do you not believe Me? He who is of God hears the words of God. For this cause you don't hear, because you are not of God."

Then the Jews answered Him, "Don't we say well that You are a Samaritan, and have a demon?"

Jesus answered, "I don't have a demon, but I honor My Father, and you dishonor Me. But I don't seek My own glory. There is One who seeks and judges. Most assuredly, I tell you, if a person keeps My word, he will never see death."

Then the Jews said to Him, "Now we know that You have a demon. Abraham died, and the prophets; and You say, 'If a man keeps My word, he will never taste of death.' Are You greater than our father, Abraham, who died? The prophets died. Who do You make Yourself out to be?"

Jesus answered, "If I glorify Myself, My glory is nothing. It is My Father Who glorifies Me, of Whom you say that He is our God. You have not known Him, but I know Him. If I said, 'I don't know Him,' I would be like you, a liar. But I know Him, and keep His word. Your father Abraham rejoiced to see My day. He saw it, and was glad."

The Jews therefore said to Him, "You are not yet fifty years old, and have You seen Abraham?"

Jesus said to them, "Most assuredly, I tell you, before Abraham came into existence, I AM." Therefore they took up stones to throw at Him, but Jesus was hidden, and went out of the temple, having gone through the midst of them, and so passed by.

COMMISSIONING OF THE SEVENTY
Luke 10:1-16

Now after these things, the Lord also appointed seventy others, and sent them two by two ahead of Him into every city and place, where He was about to come. Then He said to them, "The harvest is indeed plentiful, but the laborers are few. Pray therefore to the Lord of the harvest, that He may send out laborers into His harvest. Go your ways. Behold, I send you out as lambs among wolves. Carry no purse, nor wallet, nor sandals. Greet no one on the way.

"Into whatever house you enter, first say, 'Peace be to this house.' If a son of peace is there, your peace will rest on him; but if not, it will return to you. Remain in that same house, eating and drinking the things they give, for the laborer is worthy of his wages. Don't go from house to house.

"Into whatever city you enter, and they receive you, eat the things that are set before you. Heal the sick who are therein, and tell them, 'The Kingdom of God has come near to you.' But into whatever city you enter, and they don't receive you, go out into the streets of it and say, 'Even the dust from your city that clings to us, we wipe off against you. Nevertheless know this, that the Kingdom of God has come near to you.' I tell you, it will be more tolerable in that day for Sodom than for that city.

"Woe to you, Chorazin! Woe to you, Bethsaida! For if the mighty works had been done in Tyre and Sidon which were done in you, they would have repented long ago, sitting in sackcloth and ashes. But it will be more tolerable for Tyre and Sidon in the judgment than for you. You, Capernaum, who are exalted to Heaven, will be brought down to Hades.

"Whoever listens to you listens to Me, and whoever rejects you rejects Me. Whoever rejects Me rejects Him Who sent Me."

RETURN OF THE SEVENTY
Luke 10:17-24

The seventy returned with joy, saying, "Lord, even the demons are subject to us in Your name!"

He said to them, "I saw Satan having fallen like lightning from Heaven. Behold, I give you authority to tread on serpents and scorpions, and over all the power of the enemy. Nothing will in any way hurt you. Nevertheless, don't rejoice in this, that the spirits are subject to you, but rejoice that your names are written in Heaven."

In that same hour Jesus rejoiced in the Holy Spirit, and said, "I thank you, O Father, Lord of Heaven and earth, that You have hidden these things from the wise and understanding, and revealed them to little children. Yes, Father, for so it was well-pleasing in Your sight."

Turning to the disciples, He said, "All things have been delivered to Me by My Father. No one knows Who the Son is, except the Father, and Who the Father is, except the Son, and he to whomever the Son desires to reveal Him."

Turning to the disciples, He said privately, "Blessed are the eyes which see the things that you see, for I tell you that many prophets and kings desired to see the things which you see, and didn't see them, and to hear the things which you hear, and didn't hear them."

THE GOOD SAMARITAN
Luke 10:25-37

Behold, a certain Lawyer stood up and tested Him, saying, "Teacher, what shall I do to inherit eternal life?"

He said to him, "What is written in the law? How do you read it?"

He answered, "You shall love the Lord your God with all your heart, with all your soul, with all your strength, and with all your mind; and your neighbor as yourself."

He said to him, "You have answered correctly. Do this, and you will live."

But he, desiring to justify himself, asked Jesus, "Who is my neighbor?"

Jesus answered, "A certain man was going down from Jerusalem to Jericho, and he fell among robbers, who both stripped him and beat him, and departed, leaving him half dead. By chance a certain priest was going down that way. When he saw him, he passed by on the other side. In the same way a Levite also, when he came to the place, and saw him, passed by on the other side. But a certain Samaritan, as he traveled, came where he was. When he saw him, he was moved with compassion, came to him, and bound up his wounds, pouring on oil and wine. He set him on his own animal, and brought him to an inn, and took care of him. On the next day, when he departed, he took out two denarii, and gave them to the host, and said to him, 'Take care of him. Whatever you spend beyond that, I will repay you when I return.'

Now which of these three do you think seemed to be a neighbor to him who fell among the robbers?"

He said, "He who showed mercy on him."

Then Jesus said to him, "Go and do likewise."

JESUS VISITS WITH MARY AND MARTHA
Luke 10:38-42

It happened as they went on their way, He entered into a certain village, and a certain woman named Martha received Him into her house. She had a sister called Mary, who also sat at Jesus' feet, and heard His word. But Martha was distracted with much serving, and she came up to Him, and said, "Lord, don't You care that my sister left me to serve alone? Ask her therefore to help me."

Jesus answered her, "Martha, Martha, you are anxious and troubled about many things, but one thing is needed. Mary has chosen the good part, which will not be taken away from her."

LESSON ON HOW TO PRAY
PARABLE OF THE IMPORTUNATE FRIEND
Luke 11:1-13

It happened, that when He finished praying in a certain place, one of His disciples said to Him, "Lord, teach us to pray, just as John also taught his disciples."

He said to them, "When you pray, say,

'Our Father in Heaven, May Your name be kept holy.
May Your Kingdom come.
May Your will be done on earth, as it is in Heaven.
Give us day by day our daily bread.
Forgive us our sins,
   for we ourselves also forgive everyone who is indebted to us.
Bring us not into temptation, But deliver us from the evil one.'"

He said to them, "Which of you, if you go to a friend at midnight, and tell him, 'Friend, lend me three loaves of bread, for a friend of mine has come to me from a journey, and I have nothing to set before him,'

Then he from within will answer and say, 'Don't bother me. The door is now shut, and my children are with me in bed. I can't get up and give it to you'? I tell you, although he will not rise and give it to him because he is his friend, yet because of his persistence, he will get up and give him as many as he needs.

"I tell you, keep asking, and it will be given you. Keep seeking, and you will find. Keep knocking, and it will be opened to you. For everyone who asks receives. He who seeks finds. To him who knocks it will be opened.

"Which of you fathers, if your son asks for bread, will give him a stone? Or if he asks for a fish, he won't give him a snake instead of a fish, will he? Or if he asks for an egg, he won't give him a scorpion, will he? If you then, being evil, know how to give good gifts to your children, how much more will your Heavenly Father give the Holy Spirit to those who ask Him?"

ANOTHER BLASPHEMOUS ACCUSATION
ANOTHER DEBATE
Luke 11:14-36

He was casting out a demon, and it was mute. It happened, when the demon had gone out, the mute man spoke; and the multitudes marveled. But some of them said, "He casts out demons by Beelzebul, the prince of the demons." Others, testing Him, sought from Him a sign from Heaven.

But He, knowing their thoughts, said to them, "Every kingdom divided against itself is brought to desolation. A house divided against itself falls. If Satan also is divided against himself, how will his kingdom stand? For you say that I cast out demons by Beelzebul. But if I cast out demons by Beelzebul, by whom do your children cast them out? Therefore will they be your judges. But if I by the finger of God cast out demons, then the Kingdom of God has come to you.

"When the strong man, fully armed, guards his own dwelling, his goods are safe. But when someone stronger attacks him and overcomes him, he takes from him his whole armor in which he trusted, and divides his spoils.

"He that is not with Me is against Me. He who doesn't gather with Me scatters.

"The unclean spirit, when he has gone out of the man, passes through dry places, seeking rest, and finding none, he says, 'I will turn back to my house from which I came out.' When he returns, he finds it swept and put in order. Then he goes, and takes seven other spirits more evil than himself, and they enter in and dwell there. The last state of that man becomes worse than the first."

It came to pass, as He said these things, a certain woman out of the multitude lifted up her voice, and said to Him, "Blessed is the womb that bore You, and the breasts which nursed You!"

But He said, "On the contrary, blessed are those who hear the word of God, and keep it."

When the multitudes were gathering together to Him, He began to say, "This is an evil generation. It seeks after a sign. No sign will be given to it but the sign of Jonah, the prophet. For even as Jonah became a sign to the Ninevites, so will also the Son of Man be to this generation. The Queen of the South will rise up in the judgment with the men of this generation, and will condemn them: for she came from the ends of the earth to hear the wisdom of Solomon; and behold, One greater than Solomon is here. The men of Nineveh will stand up in the judgment with this generation, and will condemn it: for they repented at the preaching of Jonah, and behold, One greater than Jonah is here.

"No man, when he has lit a lamp, puts it in a cellar, nor under a basket, but on a stand, that those who enter in may see the light. The lamp of the body is the eye. Therefore when your eye is good, your whole body is also full of light; but when it is evil, your body also is full of darkness. Therefore see whether the light that is in you isn't darkness. If therefore your whole body is full of light, having no part dark, it will be wholly full of light, as when the lamp with its bright shining gives you light."

WOES TO THE SCRIBES AND PHARISEES
Luke 11:37-54

Now as He spoke, a certain Pharisee asked Him to dine with him. He went in, and sat at the table. When the Pharisee saw it, he marveled that He had not first washed Himself before dinner.

The Lord said to him, "Now you Pharisees cleanse the outside of the cup and of the platter, but your inward part is full of extortion and wickedness. You foolish ones, didn't He Who made the outside make the inside also? But give for gifts to the needy those things which are within, and behold, all things will be clean to you.

"But woe to you Pharisees! For you tithe mint and rue and every herb, but you bypass justice and the love of God. You ought to have done these, and not to have left the other undone.

"Woe to you Pharisees! For you love the best seats in the synagogues, and the greetings in the marketplaces.

"Woe to you, Scribes and Pharisees, hypocrites! For you are like hidden graves, and the men who walk over them don't know it."

One of the Lawyers answered Him, "Teacher, in saying this you insult us also."

He said, "Woe to you Lawyers also! For you load men with burdens that are difficult to carry, and you yourselves won't even lift one finger to help carry those burdens.

"Woe to you! For you build the tombs of the prophets, and your fathers killed them. So you testify and consent to the works of your fathers. For they killed them, and you build their tombs. Therefore also the wisdom of God said, 'I will send to them prophets and apostles; and some of them they will kill and persecute, that the blood of all the prophets, which was shed from the foundation of the world, may be required of this generation; from the blood of Abel to the blood of Zachariah, who perished between the altar and the sanctuary.' Yes, I tell you, it will be required of this generation.

"Woe to you Lawyers! For you took away the key of knowledge. You didn't enter in yourselves, and those who were entering in, you hindered."

As He said these things to them, the Scribes and the Pharisees began to be terribly angry, and to draw many things out of Him; lying in wait for Him, and seeking to catch Him in something He might say, that they might accuse Him.

WARNINGS TO THE DISCIPLES ABOUT HYPOCRISY
Luke 12:1-12

Meanwhile, when a multitude of many thousands had gathered together, so much so that they trampled on each other, He began to tell His disciples first of all, "Beware of the yeast of the Pharisees, which is hypocrisy. But there is nothing covered up, that will not be revealed, nor hidden, that will not be known. Therefore whatever you have said in the darkness will be heard in the light. What you have spoken in the ear in the inner chambers will be proclaimed on the housetops.

"I tell you, My friends, don't be afraid of those who kill the body, and after that have no more that they can do. But I will warn you Whom you should fear. Fear Him, Who after He has killed, has power to cast into Gehenna. Yes, I tell you, fear Him. Aren't five sparrows sold for two assaria coins? Not one of them is forgotten by God. But the very hairs of your head are all numbered. Therefore don't be afraid. You are of more value than many sparrows.

"I tell you, everyone who confesses Me before men, him will the Son of Man also confess before the angels of God; but he who denies Me in the presence of men will be denied in the presence of the angels of God. Everyone who speaks a word against the Son of Man will be forgiven, but those who blaspheme against the Holy Spirit will not be forgiven.

"When they bring you before the synagogues, the rulers, and the authorities, don't be anxious how or what you will answer, or what you will say; for the Holy Spirit will teach you in that same hour what you must say."

WARNINGS ABOUT GREED AND WEALTH
Luke 12:13-34

One of the multitude said to Him, "Teacher, tell my brother to divide the inheritance with me."

But He said to him, "Man, who made Me a judge or an arbitrator over you?"

90

He said to them, "Beware! Keep yourselves from covetousness, for a man's life doesn't consist of the abundance of the things which he possesses."

He spoke a parable to them, saying, "The ground of a certain rich man brought forth abundantly. He reasoned within himself, saying, 'What will I do, because I don't have room to store my crops?'

"He said, 'This is what I will do. I will pull down my barns, and build bigger ones, and there I will store all my grain and my goods. I will tell my soul, "Soul, you have many goods laid up for many years. Take your ease, eat, drink, be merry."'

"But God said to him, 'You foolish one, tonight your soul is required of you. The things which you have prepared -- whose will they be?'

"So is he who lays up treasure for himself, and is not rich toward God."

He said to His disciples, "Therefore I tell you, don't be anxious for your life, what you will eat, nor yet for your body, what you will wear. Life is more than food, and the body is more than clothing. Consider the ravens: they don't sow, they don't reap, they have no warehouse or barn, and God feeds them. How much more valuable are you than birds! Which of you by being anxious can add a cubit to his height? If then you aren't able to do even the least things, why are you anxious about the rest?

"Consider the lilies, how they grow. They don't toil, neither do they spin; yet I tell you, even Solomon in all his glory was not arrayed like one of these. But if this is how God clothes the grass in the field, which today exists, and tomorrow is cast into the oven, how much more will He clothe you, O you of little faith? Don't seek what you will eat or what you will drink; neither be anxious. For the nations of the world seek after all of these things, but your Father knows that you need these things. But seek God's Kingdom, and all these things will be added to you.

"Don't be afraid, little flock, for it is your Father's good pleasure to give you the Kingdom. Sell that which you have, and give gifts to the needy. Make for yourselves purses which don't grow old, a treasure in the heavens that doesn't fail, where no thief approaches, neither moth destroys. For where your treasure is, there will your heart be also.

WARNINGS CONCERNING THE SECOND COMING
Luke 12:35-48

"Let your loins be girded and your lamps burning. Be like men watching for their lord, when he returns from the marriage feast; that, when he comes and knocks, they may immediately open to him. Blessed are those servants, whom the lord will find watching when he comes. Most assuredly I tell you, that he will dress himself, and make them recline, and will come and serve them. They will be blessed if he comes in the second or third watch, and finds them so. But know this, that if the master of the house had known in what hour the thief was coming, he would have watched, and not allowed his house to be broken into. Therefore be ready also, for the Son of Man is coming in an hour that you don't expect Him."

Peter said to Him, "Lord, are You telling this parable to us, or to everybody?"

The Lord said, "Who then is the faithful and wise steward, whom his lord will set over his household, to give them their portion of food at the right times? Blessed is that servant whom his lord will find doing so when he comes. Truly I tell you, that he will set him over all that he has. But if that servant says in his heart, 'My lord delays his coming,' and begins to beat the menservants and the maidservants, and to eat and drink, and to be drunken, then the lord of that servant will come in a day when he isn't expecting him, and in an hour that he doesn't know, and will cut him in two, and place his portion with the unfaithful.

"That servant, who knew his lord's will, and didn't prepare, nor do what he wanted, will be beaten with many stripes, but he who didn't know, and did things worthy of stripes, will be beaten with few stripes. To whoever much is given, of him will much be required; and to whom much was entrusted, of him more will be asked.

WARNINGS ABOUT COMING DIVISIONS
Luke 12:49-53

"I came to throw fire on the earth. I wish it were already kindled. But I have a baptism to be baptized with, and how distressed I am until it is accomplished! Do you think that I have come to give peace in the earth? I tell you, no, but rather division. For from now on, there will be five in one house divided, three against two, and two against three. They will be divided, father against son, and son against father; mother against daughter, and daughter against her mother; mother-in-law against her daughter-in-law, and daughter-in-law against her mother-in-law."

THE SIGNS OF THE TIMES
Luke 12:54-59

He said to the multitudes also, "When you see a cloud rising from the west, immediately you say, 'A shower is coming,' and so it happens. When a south wind blows, you say, 'There will be a scorching heat,' and it happens. You hypocrites! You know how to interpret the appearance of the earth and the sky, but how is it that you don't interpret this time?

"Why don't you judge for yourselves what is right? For when you are going with your adversary before the magistrate, try diligently on the way to be released from him, lest perhaps he drag you to the judge, and the judge deliver you to the officer, and the officer throw you into prison. I tell you, you will by no means get out of there, until you have paid the very last penny."

REPENT OR PERISH
Luke 13:1-9

Now there were some present at the same time who told Him about the Galileans, whose blood Pilate had mixed with their sacrifices. Jesus answered them,

"Do you think that these Galileans were worse sinners than all the other Galileans, because they suffered such things? I tell you, no, but, unless you repent, you will all perish in the same way. Or those eighteen, on whom the tower in Siloam fell, and killed them; do you think that they were worse offenders than all the men who dwell in Jerusalem? I tell you, no, but, unless you repent, you will all perish in the same way."

He spoke this parable. "A certain man had a fig tree planted in his vineyard, and he came seeking fruit on it, and found none. He said to the vine dresser, 'Behold, these three years I have come looking for fruit on this fig tree, and found none. Cut it down. Why does it waste the soil?'

He answered, 'Lord, leave it alone this year also, until I dig around it, and fertilize it. If it bears fruit, fine; but if not, after that, you can cut it down.'"

OPPOSITION FOR HEALING A WOMAN ON THE SABBATH
Luke 13:10-21

He was teaching in one of the synagogues on the Sabbath day. Behold, there was a woman who had a spirit of infirmity eighteen years, and she was bent over, and could in no way straighten herself up. When Jesus saw her, He called her, and said to her, "Woman, you are freed from your infirmity." He laid His hands on her, and immediately she stood up straight, and glorified God.

The ruler of the synagogue, being indignant because Jesus had healed on the Sabbath, said to the multitude, "There are six days in which men ought to work. Therefore come on those days and be healed, and not on the Sabbath day!"

Therefore the Lord answered him, "You hypocrites! Doesn't each one of you free his ox or his donkey from the stall on the Sabbath, and lead him away to water? Ought not this woman, being a daughter of Abraham, whom Satan had bound eighteen long years, be freed from this bondage on the Sabbath day?"

As He said these things, all His adversaries were disappointed, and all the multitude rejoiced for all the glorious things that were done by Him.

He said, "What is the Kingdom of God like? To what shall I compare it? It is like a grain of mustard seed, which a man took, and put in his own garden. It grew, and became a large tree, and the birds of the sky lodged in its branches."

Again He said, "To what shall I compare the Kingdom of God? It is like yeast, which a woman took and hid in three measures of flour, until it was all leavened."

THE HEALING OF THE BLIND MAN
John 9:1-41

As He passed by, He saw a man blind from birth. His disciples asked Him, "Rabbi, who sinned, this man or his parents, that he was born blind?"

Jesus answered, "Neither did this man sin, nor his parents; but, that the works of God might be revealed in him. I must work the works of Him Who sent Me, while it is day. The night is coming, when no one can work. While I am in the world, I am the Light of the world."

When He had said this, He spat on the ground, made mud with the saliva, anointed the blind man's eyes with the mud, and said to him, "Go, wash in the pool of Siloam" (which means "Sent"). So he went away, washed, and came back seeing.

The neighbors therefore, and those who saw that he was blind before, said, "Isn't this he who sat and begged?"

Others were saying, "It is he."

Still others were saying, "He looks like him."

He said, "I am he."

They therefore were asking him, "How were your eyes opened?"

He answered, "A man called Jesus made mud, anointed my eyes, and said to me, 'Go to the pool of Siloam, and wash.' So I went away and washed, and I received sight."

Then they asked him, "Where is He?"

He said, "I don't know."

They brought him who had been blind to the Pharisees. It was a Sabbath when Jesus made the mud and opened his eyes. Again therefore the Pharisees also asked him how he received his sight. He said to them, "He put mud on my eyes, I washed, and I see."

Some therefore of the Pharisees said, "This man is not from God, because He doesn't keep the Sabbath."

Others said, "How can a man who is a sinner do such signs?" There was division among them.

Therefore they asked the blind man again, "What do you say about Him, because He opened your eyes?"

He said, "He is a prophet."

The Jews therefore did not believe concerning him, that he had been blind, and had received his sight, until they called the parents of him who had received his sight, and asked them, "Is this your son, who you say was born blind? How then does he now see?"

His parents answered them, "We know that this is our son, and that he was born blind; but how he now sees, we don't know; or who opened his eyes, we don't know. He is of age. Ask him. He will speak for himself." His parents said these things because they feared the Jews; for the Jews had already agreed that if any man would confess Him as Christ, he would be put out of the synagogue. Therefore his parents said, "He is of age. Ask him."

So they called the man who was blind a second time, and said to him, "Give glory to God. We know that this man is a sinner."

He therefore answered, "I don't know if He is a sinner. One thing I do know: that though I was blind, now I see."

They said to him again, "What did He do to you? How did He open your eyes?"

He answered them, "I told you already, and you didn't listen. Why do you want to hear it again? You don't also want to become His disciples, do you?"

They insulted him and said, "You are His disciple, but we are disciples of Moses. We know that God has spoken to Moses. But as for this man, we don't know where He comes from."

The man answered them, "How amazing! You don't know where He comes from, yet He opened my eyes. We know that God doesn't listen to sinners, but if anyone is a worshipper of God, and does His will, He listens to him. Since the world began it has never been heard of that anyone opened the eyes of someone born blind. If this man were not from God, He could do nothing."

They answered him, "You were altogether born in sins, and do you teach us?" They threw him out.

Jesus heard that they had thrown him out, and finding him, He said, "Do you believe in the Son of God?"

He answered, "Who is He, Lord, that I may believe in Him?"

Jesus said to him, "You have both seen Him, and it is He Who speaks with you."

He said, "Lord, I believe!" and he worshiped Him.

Jesus said, "I came into this world for judgment, that those who don't see may see; and that those who see may become blind."

Those of the Pharisees who were with Him heard these things, and said to Him, "Are we also blind?"

Jesus said to them, "If you were blind, you would have no sin; but now you say, 'We see.' Therefore your sin remains.

THE GOOD SHEPHERD AND THE THIEF
John 10:1-18

"Most assuredly, I tell you, one who doesn't enter by the door into the sheep fold, but climbs up some other way, the same is a thief and a robber. But one who enters in by the door is the shepherd of the sheep. The gatekeeper opens the gate for him, and the sheep listen to his voice. He calls his own sheep by name, and leads them out. Whenever he brings out his own sheep, he goes before them, and the sheep follow him, for they know his voice. They will by no means follow a stranger, but will flee from him; for they don't know the voice of strangers." Jesus spoke this parable to them, but they didn't understand what He was telling them.

"Jesus therefore said to them again, "Most assuredly, I tell you, I am the sheep's door. All who came before Me are thieves and robbers, but the sheep didn't listen to them. I am the door. If anyone enters in by Me, he will be saved, and will go in and go out, and will find pasture. The thief only comes to steal, kill, and destroy. I came that they may have life, and may have it abundantly.

"I am the good shepherd. The good shepherd lays down His life for the sheep. He who is a hired hand, and not a shepherd, who doesn't own the sheep, sees the wolf coming, leaves the sheep, and flees. The wolf snatches the sheep, and scatters them. The hired hand flees because he is a hired hand, and doesn't care for the sheep.

"I am the good shepherd. I know My own, and I'm known by My own; even as the Father knows Me, and I know the Father. I lay down My life for the sheep. I have other sheep, which are not of this fold. I must bring them also, and they will hear My voice. They will become one flock with one shepherd. Therefore the Father loves Me, because I lay down My life, that I may take it again. No one takes it away from Me, but I lay it down by Myself. I have power to lay it down, and I have power to take it again. I received this commandment from My Father."

MORE DIVISIONS AMONG THE JEWS
ANOTHER ATTEMPT TO ARREST JESUS
John 10:19-39

Therefore a division arose again among the Jews because of these words. Many of them said, "He has a demon, and is insane! Why do you listen to Him?"

Others said, "These are not the sayings of one possessed by a demon. It isn't possible for a demon to open the eyes of the blind, is it?"

It was the Feast of the Dedication at Jerusalem. It was winter, and Jesus was walking in the temple, in Solomon's porch. The Jews therefore came around Him and said to Him, "How long will You hold us in suspense? If You are the Christ, tell us plainly."

Jesus answered them, "I told you, and you don't believe. The works that I do in My Father's name, these testify about Me. But you don't believe, because you are not of My sheep, as I told you. My sheep hear My voice, and I know them, and they follow Me. I give eternal life to them. They will never perish, and no one will snatch them out of My hand. My Father, Who has given them to Me, is greater than all. No one is able to snatch them out of My Father's hand. I and the Father are one."

Therefore Jews took up stones again to stone Him. Jesus answered them, "I have shown you many good works from My Father. For which of those works do you stone Me?"

The Jews answered him, "We don't stone You for a good work, but for blasphemy: because You, being a man, make Yourself God."

Jesus answered them, "Isn't it written in your law,

'I said, you are gods?'

"If He called them gods, to whom the word of God came (and the Scripture can't be broken), do you say of Him Whom the Father sanctified and sent into the world, 'You blaspheme,' because I said, 'I am the Son of God?' If I don't do the works of My Father, don't believe Me. But if I do them, though you don't believe Me, believe the works; that you may know and believe that the Father is in Me, and I in the Father." They sought again to seize Him, and He went out of their hand.

JESUS GOES BACK ACROSS THE JORDAN
John 10:40-42

He went away again beyond the Jordan into the place where John was baptizing at first, and there He stayed. Many came to Him. They said, "John indeed did no sign, but everything that John said about this man is true." Many believed in Him there.

QUESTIONS ABOUT SALVATION AND THE KINGDOM
Luke 13:22-30

He went on His way through cities and villages, teaching, and traveling on to Jerusalem. One said to Him, "Lord, are they few who are saved?"

He said to them, "Strive to enter in by the narrow door, for many, I tell you, will seek to enter in, and will not be able. When once the master of the house has risen up, and has shut the door, and you begin to stand outside, and to knock at the door, saying, 'Lord, lord, open to us!'

"Then He will answer and tell you, 'I don't know you or where you come from.'

"Then you will begin to say, 'We ate and drank in Your presence, and You taught in our streets.'

"He will say, 'I tell you, I don't know where you come from. Depart from Me, all you workers of iniquity.'

"There will be weeping and gnashing of teeth, when you see Abraham, Isaac, Jacob, and all the prophets, in the Kingdom of God, and yourselves being thrown outside. They will come from the east, west, north, and south, and will sit down in the Kingdom of God. Behold, there are some who are last who will be first, and there are some who are first who will be last."

JESUS' COMING DEATH AND LAMENT OVER JERUSALEM
Luke 13:31-35

On that same day, some Pharisees came, saying to Him, "Get out of here, and go away, for Herod wants to kill You."

He said to them, "Go and tell that fox, 'Behold, I cast out demons and perform cures today and tomorrow, and the third day I complete My mission. Nevertheless I must go on My way today and tomorrow and the next day, for it can't be that a prophet perish outside of Jerusalem.'

"Jerusalem, Jerusalem, that kills the prophets, and stones those who are sent to her! How often I wanted to gather your children together, like a hen gathers her own brood under her wings, and you refused! Behold, your house is left to you desolate. I tell you, you will not see Me, until you say, 'Blessed is He Who comes in the name of the Lord!'"

HEALING OF A MAN WITH DROPSY
Luke 14:1-24

It happened, when He went into the house of one of the rulers of the Pharisees on a Sabbath to eat bread, that they were watching Him. Behold, a certain man who had dropsy was in front of Him. Jesus, answering, spoke to the Lawyers and Pharisees, saying, "Is it lawful to heal on the Sabbath?" But they were silent. He took him, and healed him, and let him go.

He answered them, "Which of you, if your son or an ox fell into a well, wouldn't immediately pull him out on a Sabbath day?" They couldn't answer Him regarding these things.

He spoke a parable to those who were invited, when He noticed how they chose the best seats, and said to them, "When you are invited by anyone to a marriage feast, don't sit in the best seat, since perhaps someone more honorable than you might be invited by him, and he who invited both of you would come and tell you, 'Make room for this person.' Then you would begin, with shame, to take the lowest place. But when you are invited, go and sit in the lowest place, so that when he who invited you comes, he may tell you, 'Friend, move up higher.' Then you will be honored in the presence of all who sit at the table with you. For everyone who exalts himself will be humbled, and whoever humbles himself will be exalted."

He also said to the one who had invited Him, "When you make a dinner or a supper, don't call your friends, nor your brothers, nor your kinsmen, nor rich neighbors, or perhaps they might also return the favor, and pay you back. But when you make a feast, ask the poor, the maimed, the lame, or the blind; and you will be blessed, because they don't have the resources to repay you. For you will be repaid in the resurrection of the righteous."

When one of those who sat at the table with Him heard these things, he said to Him, "Blessed is he who will feast in the Kingdom of God!"

But He said to him, "A certain man made a great supper, and he invited many people. He sent out his servant at supper time to tell those who were invited, 'Come, for everything is ready now.'

"They all as one began to make excuses. "The first said to him, 'I have bought a field, and I must go and see it. Please have me excused.'

"Another said, 'I have bought five yoke of oxen, and I must go try them out. Please have me excused.'

"Another said, 'I have married a wife, and therefore I can't come.'

"That servant came, and told his lord these things. Then the master of the house, being angry, said to his servant, 'Go out quickly into the streets and lanes of the city, and bring in the poor, maimed, blind, and lame.'

"The servant said, 'Lord, it is done as you commanded, and there is still room.'

"The lord said to the servant, 'Go out into the highways and hedges, and compel them to come in, that my house may be filled. For I tell you that none of those men who were invited will taste of my supper.'"

THE COST OF DISCIPLESHIP
Luke 14:25-35

Now great multitudes were going with Him. He turned and said to them, "If anyone comes to Me, and doesn't hate his own father, mother, wife, children, brothers, and sisters, yes, and his own life also, he can't be My disciple. Whoever doesn't bear his own cross, and come after Me, can't be My disciple.

"For which of you, desiring to build a tower, doesn't first sit down and count the cost, to see if he has enough to complete it? Or perhaps, when he has laid a foundation, and is not able to finish, everyone who sees begins to mock him, saying, 'This man began to build, and wasn't able to finish.'

"Or what king, as he goes to encounter another king in war, will not sit down first and consider whether he is able with ten thousand to meet him who comes against him with twenty thousand? Or else, while the other is yet a great way off, he sends an envoy, and asks for conditions of peace. So therefore whoever of you who doesn't renounce all that he has, he can't be My disciple.

"Salt is good, but if the salt becomes flat and tasteless, with what do you season it? It is fit neither for the soil nor for the manure pile. It is thrown out.

"He who has ears to hear, let him hear."

THE LOST SHEEP, THE LOST COIN, THE LOST SON
Luke 15:1-32

Now all the tax collectors and sinners were coming close to Him to hear Him. The Pharisees and the Scribes murmured, saying, "This man welcomes sinners, and eats with them."

He told them this parable. "Which of you men, if you had one hundred sheep, and lost one of them, wouldn't leave the ninety-nine in the wilderness, and go after the one that was lost, until he found it? When he has found it, he carries it on his shoulders, rejoicing. When he comes home, he calls together his friends and his neighbors, saying to them, 'Rejoice with me, for I have found my sheep which was lost!' I tell you that even so there will be more joy in Heaven over one sinner who repents, than over ninety-nine righteous people who need no repentance.

"Or what woman, if she had ten drachma coins, if she lost one drachma coin, wouldn't light a lamp, sweep the house, and seek diligently until she found it? When she has found it, she calls together her friends and neighbors, saying, 'Rejoice with me, for I have found the drachma which I had lost.' Even so, I tell you, there is joy in the presence of the angels of God over one sinner repenting."

He said, "A certain man had two sons. The younger of them said to his father, 'Father, give me my share of your property.' He divided his livelihood between them.

"Not many days after, the younger son gathered all of this together and traveled into a far country. There he wasted his property with riotous living. When he had spent all of it, there arose a severe famine in that country, and he began to be in need. He went and joined himself to one of the citizens of that country, and he sent him into his fields to feed pigs. He wanted to fill his belly with the husks that the pigs ate, but no one gave him anything.

"But when he came to himself he said, 'How many hired servants of my father's have bread enough to spare, and I'm dying with hunger! I will get up and go to my father, and will tell him, "Father, I have sinned against Heaven, and in your sight. I am no more worthy to be called your son. Make me as one of your hired servants."'

"He arose, and came to his father. But while he was still far off, his father saw him, and was moved with compassion, and ran, and fell on his neck, and kissed him.

"The son said to him, 'Father, I have sinned against Heaven, and in your sight. I am no longer worthy to be called your son.'

"But the father said to his servants, 'Bring out the best robe, and put it on him. Put a ring on his hand, and shoes on his feet. Bring the fattened calf, kill it, and let us eat, and celebrate; for this, my son, was dead, and is alive again. He was lost, and is found.' They began to celebrate.

"Now his elder son was in the field. As he came near to the house, he heard music and dancing. He called one of the servants to him, and asked what was going on. He said to him, 'Your brother has come, and your father has killed the fattened calf, because he has received him back safe and healthy.'

"But he was angry, and would not go in. Therefore his father came out, and begged him. But he answered his father, 'Behold, these many years I have served you, and I never disobeyed a commandment of yours, but you never gave me a goat, that I might celebrate with my friends. But when this, your son, came, who has devoured your living with prostitutes, you killed the fattened calf for him.'

"He said to him, 'Son, you are always with me, and all that is mine is yours. But it was appropriate to celebrate and be glad, for this, your brother, was dead, and is alive again. He was lost, and is found.'"

THE SHREWD MANAGER
Luke 16:1-13

He also said to His disciples, "There was a certain rich man who had a manager. An accusation was made to him that this man was wasting his possessions. He called him, and said to him, 'What is this that I hear about you? Give an accounting of your management, for you can no longer be manager.'

"The manager said within himself, 'What will I do, seeing that my lord is taking away the management position from me? I don't have strength to dig. I am ashamed to beg. I know what I will do, so that when I am removed from management, they may receive me into their houses.'

"Calling each one of his lord's debtors to him, he said to the first, 'How much do you owe to my lord?'

"He said, 'A hundred batos of oil.'

"He said to him, 'Take your bill, and sit down quickly and write fifty.'

"Then said he to another, 'How much do you owe?'

"He said, 'A hundred cors of wheat.' He said to him, 'Take your bill, and write eighty.'

"His lord commended the dishonest manager because he had done wisely, for the children of this world are, in their own generation, wiser than the children of the light. I tell you, make for yourselves friends by means of unrighteous mammon, so that when you fail, they may receive you into the eternal tents.

"He who is faithful in a very little is faithful also in much. He who is dishonest in a very little is also dishonest in much. If therefore you have not been faithful in the unrighteous mammon, who will commit to your trust the true riches? If you have not been faithful in that which is another's, who will give you that which is your own?

"No servant can serve two masters, for either he will hate the one, and love the other; or else he will hold to one, and despise the other. You aren't able to serve God and mammon."

THE RICH MAN AND LAZARUS
Luke 16:14-31

The Pharisees, who were lovers of money, also heard all these things, and they scoffed at Him. He said to them, "You are those who justify yourselves in the sight of men, but God knows your hearts. For that which is exalted among men is an abomination in the sight of God.

"The law and the prophets were until John. From that time the gospel of the Kingdom of God is preached, and everyone is forcing his way into it. But it is easier for Heaven and earth to pass away, than for one tiny stroke of a pen in the law to fall.

"Everyone who divorces his wife, and marries another, commits adultery. He who marries one who is divorced from a husband commits adultery.

"Now there was a certain rich man, and he was clothed in purple and fine linen, living in luxury every day. A certain beggar, named Lazarus, was laid at his gate, full of sores, and desiring to be fed with the crumbs that fell from the rich man's table. Yes, even the dogs came and licked his sores.

"It happened that the beggar died, and that he was carried away by the angels to Abraham's bosom. The rich man also died, and was buried. In Hades, he lifted up his eyes, being in torment, and saw Abraham far off, and Lazarus at his bosom. He cried and said, 'Father Abraham, have mercy on me, and send Lazarus, that he may dip the tip of his finger in water, and cool my tongue! For I am in anguish in this flame.'

"But Abraham said, 'Son, remember that you, in your lifetime, received your good things, and Lazarus, in like manner, bad things. But now here he is comforted and you are in anguish. Besides all this, between us and you there is a great gulf fixed, that those who want to pass from here to you are not able, and that none may cross over from there to us.'

"He said, 'I ask you therefore, father, that you would send him to my father's house; for I have five brothers, that he may testify to them, so they won't also come into this place of torment.'

"But Abraham said to him, 'They have Moses and the prophets. Let them listen to them.'

"He said, 'No, father Abraham, but if one goes to them from the dead, they will repent.'

"He said to him, 'If they don't listen to Moses and the prophets, neither will they be persuaded if one rises from the dead.'"

SIN, FAITH, AND DUTY
Luke 17:1-10

He said to the disciples, "It is impossible that no occasions of stumbling should come, but woe to him through whom they come! It would be better for him if a millstone were hung around his neck, and he were thrown into the sea, rather than that he should cause one of these little ones to stumble. Be careful.

"If your brother sins against you, rebuke him. If he repents, forgive him. If he sins against you seven times in the day, and seven times returns, saying, 'I repent,' you shall forgive him."

The apostles said to the Lord, "Increase our faith."

The Lord said, "If you had faith like a grain of mustard seed, you would tell this sycamore tree, 'Be uprooted, and be planted in the sea,' and it would obey you.

"But who is there among you, having a servant plowing or keeping sheep, that will say, when he comes in from the field, 'Come immediately and sit down at the table,' and will not rather tell him, 'Prepare my supper, clothe yourself properly, and serve me, while I eat and drink. Afterward you shall eat and drink'? Does he thank that servant because he did the things that were commanded? I think not. Even so you also, when you have done all the things that are commanded you, say, 'We are unworthy servants. We have done our duty.'"

THE SICKNESS AND DEATH OF LAZARUS
John 11:1-16

Now a certain man was sick, Lazarus from Bethany, of the village of Mary and her sister, Martha. It was that Mary who had anointed the Lord with ointment, and wiped His feet with her hair, whose brother, Lazarus, was sick. The sisters therefore sent to Him, saying, "Lord, behold, he for whom You have great affection is sick."

But when Jesus heard it, He said, "This sickness is not to death, but for the glory of God, that God's Son may be glorified by it." Now Jesus loved Martha, and her sister, and Lazarus. When therefore He heard that he was sick, He stayed two days in the place where He was.

Then after this He said to the disciples, "Let's go into Judea again."

The disciples told Him, "Rabbi, the Jews were just trying to stone You, and are You going there again?"

Jesus answered, "Aren't there twelve hours of daylight? If a man walks in the day, he doesn't stumble, because he sees the light of this world. But if a man walks in the night, he stumbles, because the light isn't in him."

He said these things, and after that, He said to them, "Our friend, Lazarus, has fallen asleep, but I am going so that I may awake him out of sleep."

The disciples therefore said, "Lord, if he has fallen asleep, he will recover." Now Jesus had spoken of his death, but they thought that He spoke of taking rest in sleep.

So Jesus said to them plainly then, "Lazarus is dead. I am glad for your sakes that I was not there, so that you may believe. Nevertheless, let's go to him."

Thomas therefore, who is called Didymus, said to his fellow disciples, "Let's go also, that we may die with him."

LAZARUS IS RAISED FROM THE DEAD
John 11:17-44

So when Jesus came, He found that he had been in the tomb four days already. Now Bethany was near Jerusalem, about fifteen stadia away. Many of the Jews had joined the women around Martha and Mary, to console them concerning their brother. Then when Martha heard that Jesus was coming, she went and met Him, but Mary stayed in the house.

Therefore Martha said to Jesus, "Lord, if You would have been here, my brother wouldn't have died. Even now I know that, whatever You ask of God, God will give you."

Jesus said to her, "Your brother will rise again."

Martha said to Him, "I know that he will rise again in the resurrection at the last day."

Jesus said to her, "I am the resurrection and the life. He who believes in Me, though he die, yet will he live. Whoever lives and believes in Me will never die. Do you believe this?"

She said to Him, "Yes, Lord. I have come to believe that You are the Christ, God's Son, He Who comes into the world."

When she had said this, she went away, and called Mary, her sister, secretly, saying, "The Teacher is here, and is calling you." When she heard this, she arose quickly, and went to Him. Now Jesus had not yet come into the village, but was in the place where Martha met Him. Then the Jews who were with her in the house, and were consoling her, when they saw Mary, that she rose up quickly and went out, followed her, saying, "She is going to the tomb to weep there."

Therefore when Mary came to where Jesus was, and saw Him, she fell down at His feet, saying to Him, "Lord, if You would have been here, my brother would-n't have died."

When Jesus therefore saw her weeping, and the Jews weeping who came with her, He groaned in the Spirit, and was troubled, and said, "Where have you laid him?"

They told Him, "Lord, come and see."

Jesus wept.

The Jews therefore said, "See how much affection He had for him!"

Some of them said, "Couldn't this man, Who opened the eyes of him who was blind, have also kept this man from dying?"

Jesus therefore, again groaning in Himself, came to the tomb. Now it was a cave, and a stone lay against it. Jesus said, "Take away the stone."

Martha, the sister of him who was dead, said to Him, "Lord, by this time there is a stench, for he has been dead four days."

Jesus said to her, "Didn't I tell you that if you believed, you would see God's glory?"

So they took away the stone from the place where the dead man was lying. Jesus lifted up His eyes, and said, "Father, I thank You that You listened to Me. I know that You always listen to Me, but because of the multitude that stands around I said this, that they may believe that You sent Me."

When He had said this, He cried with a loud voice, "Lazarus, come out!" He who was dead came out, bound hand and foot with wrappings, and his face was wrapped around with a cloth.

Jesus said to them, "Free him, and let him go."

THE PLOT TO KILL JESUS
John 11:45-54

Therefore many of the Jews, who came to Mary and saw what Jesus did, be-lieved in Him. But some of them went away to the Pharisees, and told them the things which Jesus had done.

The Chief Priests therefore and the Pharisees gathered a council, and said, "What are we doing? For this man does many signs. If we leave Him alone like this, everyone will believe in Him, and the Romans will come and take away both our place and our nation."

But a certain one of them, Caiaphas, being high priest that year, said to them, "You know nothing at all, nor do you consider that it is advantageous for us that one man should die for the people, and that the whole nation not perish."

Now he didn't say this of himself, but being high priest that year, he prophesied that Jesus would die for the nation, and not for the nation only, but that He might also gather together into one the children of God who are scattered abroad. So from that day forward they took counsel that they might put Him to death.

Jesus therefore walked no more openly among the Jews, but departed from there into the country near the wilderness, to a city called Ephraim. He stayed there with His disciples.

TEN LEPERS HEALED WHILE PASSING THROUGH SAMARIA
Luke 17:11-19

It happened as He was on His way to Jerusalem, that He was passing along the borders of Samaria and Galilee. As He entered into a certain village, ten men who were lepers met Him, who stood at a distance. They lifted up their voices, saying, "Jesus, Master, have mercy on us!"

When He saw them, He said to them, "Go and show yourselves to the priests." It happened that as they went, they were cleansed.

One of them, when he saw that he was healed, turned back, glorifying God with a loud voice. He fell on his face at Jesus' feet, giving Him thanks; and he was a Samaritan.

Jesus answered, "Weren't the ten cleansed? But where are the nine? Were there none found who returned to give glory to God, except this stranger?" Then He said to him, "Get up, and go your way. Your faith has healed you."

MORE ON THE COMING OF THE SON OF MAN
Luke 17:20-37

Being asked by the Pharisees when the Kingdom of God would come, He answered them, "The Kingdom of God doesn't come with observation; neither will they say, 'Look, here!' or, 'Look, there!' for behold, the Kingdom of God is within you."

He said to the disciples, "The days will come, when you will desire to see one of the days of the Son of Man, and you will not see it. They will tell you, 'Look, here!' or 'Look, there!' Don't go away, nor follow after them, for as the lightning, when it flashes out of the one part under the sky, shines to the other part under the sky; so will the Son of Man be in His day. But first, He must suffer many things and be rejected by this generation.

"As it happened in the days of Noah, even so will it be also in the days of the Son of Man. They ate, they drank, they married, they were given in marriage, until the day that Noah entered into the ark, and the flood came, and destroyed them all.

"Likewise, even as it happened in the days of Lot: they ate, they drank, they bought, they sold, they planted, they built; but in the day that Lot went out from Sodom, it rained fire and sulfur from heaven, and destroyed them all.

"It will be the same way in the day that the Son of Man is revealed. In that day, he who will be on the housetop, and his goods in the house, let him not go down to take them away. Let him who is in the field likewise not turn back. Remember Lot's wife! Whoever seeks to save his life loses it, but whoever loses his life preserves it. I tell you, in that night there will be two people in one bed. The one will be taken, and the other will be left. There will be two grinding grain together. One will be taken, and the other will be left. Two *men* shall be in the field; the one shall be taken, and the other left."

They answering, asked Him, "Where, Lord?"

He said to them, "Where the body is, there will the vultures also be gathered together."

PARABLES ON PRAYER
Luke 18:1-14

He also spoke a parable to them that they must always pray, and not give up, saying, "There was a judge in a certain city who didn't fear God, and didn't respect man. A widow was in that city, and she often came to him, saying, 'Defend me from my adversary!'

"He wouldn't for a while, but afterward he said to himself, 'Though I neither fear God, nor respect man, yet because this widow bothers me, I will defend her, or else she will wear me out by her continual coming.'"

The Lord said, "Listen to what the unrighteous judge says. Won't God avenge His elect, who are crying out to Him day and night, and yet He exercises patience with them? I tell you that He will avenge them quickly. Nevertheless, when the Son of Man comes, will He find faith on the earth?"

He spoke also this parable to certain people who were convinced of their own righteousness, and who despised all others. "Two men went up into the temple to pray; one was a Pharisee, and the other was a tax collector. The Pharisee stood and prayed to himself like this: 'God, I thank you, that I am not like the rest of men, extortioners, unrighteous, adulterers, or even like this tax collector. I fast twice a week. I give tithes of all that I get.'

"But the tax collector, standing far away, wouldn't even lift up his eyes to Heaven, but beat his breast, saying, 'God, be merciful to me, a sinner!'

"I tell you, this man went down to his house justified rather than the other; for everyone who exalts himself will be humbled, but he who humbles himself will be exalted."

DIVORCE AND REMARRIAGE
Matthew 19:1-12; Mark 10:1-12

It happened when Jesus had finished these words, He arose from there and departed from Galilee, and came into the borders of Judea beyond the Jordan. Great multitudes followed Him, and He healed them there. As He usually did, He was again teaching them.

Pharisees came to Him, testing Him, and saying, "Is it lawful for a man to divorce his wife for any reason?"

He answered, "Haven't you read that He Who made them from the beginning made them male and female, and said, 'For this cause a man shall leave his father and mother, and shall join to his wife; and the two shall become one flesh?' So that they are no more two, but one flesh. What therefore God has joined together, don't let man tear apart. What did Moses command you?"

They said, "Moses allowed a certificate of divorce to be written, and to divorce her." They then asked Him, "Why then did Moses command us to give her a bill of divorce, and divorce her?"

He said to them, "Moses, because of the hardness of your hearts, wrote you this commandment and allowed you to divorce your wives, but from the beginning of the creation it has not been so. I tell you that whoever divorces his wife, except for sexual immorality, and marries another, commits adultery; and he who marries her when she is divorced commits adultery."

In the house, His disciples asked Him again about the same matter and said to Him, "If this is the case of the man with his wife, it is not expedient to marry."

He said to them, "Whoever divorces his wife, and marries another, commits adultery against her. If a woman herself divorces her husband, and marries another, she commits adultery."

But He said to them, "Not all men can receive this saying, but those to whom it is given. For there are eunuchs who were born that way from their mother's womb, and there are eunuchs who were made eunuchs by men; and there are eunuchs who made themselves eunuchs for the Kingdom of Heaven's sake. He who is able to receive it, let him receive it."

LITTLE CHILDREN AND THE KINGDOM
Matthew 19:13-15; Mark 10:13-16; Luke 18:15-17

They were also bringing their babies and little children to Him, that He might touch them and lay His hands on them and pray. But when the disciples saw it, they rebuked them.

But when Jesus saw it, He was moved with indignation, and summoned them, saying, "Allow the little children to come to Me, and don't hinder them, for the Kingdom of God and Kingdom of Heaven belongs to such as these. Most assuredly, I tell you, whoever doesn't receive the Kingdom of God like a little child, he will in no way enter into it."

He took them in His arms, and blessed them, and He laid His hands on them, and departed from there.

RICHES AND THE KINGDOM
Matthew 19:16-30; Mark 10:17-31; Luke 18:18-30

Behold, as He was going out into the way, a certain ruler ran to Him, knelt before Him, and asked Him, saying, "Good Teacher, what good thing shall I do to inherit eternal life?"

Jesus asked him, "Why do you call Me good? No one is good, except one -- God. But if you want to enter into life, keep the commandments."

He said to Him, "Which ones?"

Jesus said, "You know the commandments: 'Don't commit adultery,' 'Don't murder,' 'Don't steal,' 'Don't give false testimony,' 'Do not defraud,' 'Honor your father and your mother and, 'You shall love your neighbor as yourself.'"

The young man said to Him, "Teacher, I have observed all these things from my youth up. What do I still lack?"

Jesus, looking at him, loved him, and He said to him, "You still lack one thing, if you want to be perfect, go, sell all that you have, and distribute it to the poor. You will have treasure in Heaven. Come, take up the cross, and follow Me."

But when he heard these things, he went away and became very sad, for he was very rich and had great possessions.

Jesus, seeing that he became very sad, said to His disciples, "Most assuredly I say to you, a rich man will enter into the Kingdom of Heaven with difficulty. How hard it is for those who have riches to enter into the Kingdom of God! For it is easier for a camel to enter in through a needle's eye, than for a rich man to enter into the Kingdom of God."

The disciples were amazed at His words. But Jesus answered again, "Children, how hard is it for those who trust in riches to enter into the Kingdom of God?"

When the disciples heard it, they were exceedingly astonished, saying, "Then who can be saved?"

Looking at them, Jesus said, "The things which are impossible with men are possible with God, for all things are possible with God."

Peter said, "Look, we have left everything, and followed you. What then will we have?"

He said to them, "Most assuredly I tell you who have followed Me, that you in the regeneration when the Son of Man will sit on the throne of His glory, you also will sit on twelve thrones, judging the twelve tribes of Israel. There is no one who has left houses, or wife, or brothers, or sisters, or parents, or children, or lands, for the Kingdom of God's sake, and for My name's sake, and for the gospel's sake, who will not receive many times more, one hundred times more, in this time, and in the world to come, eternal life. But many will be last who are first; and first who are last."

PARABLE OF THE VINEYARD
Matthew 20:1-16

"For the Kingdom of Heaven is like a man who was the master of a household, who went out early in the morning to hire laborers for his vineyard. When he had agreed with the laborers for a denarius a day, he sent them into his vineyard.

"He went out about the third hour, and saw others standing idle in the marketplace. To them he said, 'You also go into the vineyard, and whatever is right I will give you.' So they went their way.

"Again he went out about the sixth and the ninth hour, and did likewise. About the eleventh hour he went out, and found others standing idle. He said to them, 'Why do you stand here all day idle?'

"They said to him, 'Because no one has hired us.'

"He said to them, 'You also go into the vineyard, and you will receive whatever is right.'

"When evening had come, the lord of the vineyard said to his steward, 'Call the laborers and pay them their wages, beginning from the last to the first.'

"When those who were hired at about the eleventh hour came, they each received a denarius. When the first came, they supposed that they would receive more; and they likewise each received a denarius. When they received it, they murmured against the master of the household, saying, 'These last have spent one hour, and you have made them equal to us, who have borne the burden of the day and the scorching heat!'

"But he answered one of them, 'Friend, I am doing you no wrong. Didn't you agree with me for a denarius? Take that which is yours, and go your way. It is my desire to give to this last just as much as to you. Isn't it lawful for me to do what I want to with what I own? Or is your eye evil, because I am good?'

"So the last will be first, and the first last. For many are called, but few are chosen."

THIRD PREDICTION OF THE RESURRECTION
Matthew 20:17-19; Mark 10:32-34; Luke 18:31-34

As Jesus was going up to Jerusalem, He was going in front of them, and they were amazed; and those who followed were afraid. He took the twelve aside and began to tell them the things that were going to happen to Him. As they went on the way He said to them, "Behold, we are going up to Jerusalem, and all the things that are written through the prophets concerning the Son of Man will be completed. For He will be delivered up to the Chief Priests and Scribes, and to the Gentiles, and they will condemn Him to death. He will be mocked, treated shamefully, and spit on. They will scourge, crucify, and kill Him. On the third day, He will rise again." They understood none of these things. This saying was hidden from them, and they didn't understand the things that were said.

A MOTHER'S REQUEST AND AMBITIOUS PRIDE
Matthew 20:20-28; Mark 10:35-45

Then the mother of the sons of Zebedee came to Him with her sons, kneeling and asking a certain thing of Him.

Then James and John, came near to Him, saying, "Teacher, we want You to do for us whatever we will ask."

He said to them, "What do you want Me to do for you?"

The mother of the two spoke up and she said to Him, "Command that these, my two sons, may sit, one on Your right hand, and one on Your left hand, in Your Kingdom."

James and John also came nearer and spoke up and they said to Him, "Grant to us that we may sit, one at Your right hand, and one at Your left hand, in Your glory."

But Jesus answered, "You don't know what you are asking. Are you able to drink the cup that I am about to drink, and be baptized with the baptism that I am baptized with?"

They said to Him, "We are able."

He said to them, "You will indeed drink My cup, and be baptized with the baptism that I am baptized with, but to sit on My right hand and on My left hand is not Mine to give; but it is for whom it has been prepared by My Father."

When the ten heard it, they were indignant with the two brothers.

But Jesus summoned them, and said, "You know that they who are recognized as the rulers of the Gentiles lord it over them, and their great ones exercise authority over them. But it shall not be so among you, but whoever desires to become great among you shall be your servant. Whoever desires to be first among you shall be your bondservant of all. Even as the Son of Man came not to be served, but to serve, and to give His life as a ransom for many."

HEALING OF BLIND BARTIMAEUS
Matthew 20:29-34; Mark 10:46-52; Luke 18:35-43

They came to Jericho. As He went out from Jericho, with His disciples and a great multitude followed Him, two blind men were sitting by the road. One of them was the son of Timaeus, Bartimaeus, and he was a beggar. Hearing a multitude going by, he asked what this meant. They told him that Jesus of Nazareth was passing by. He cried out, "Jesus, You son of David, have mercy on me!" Then they both cried out, "Lord, have mercy on us, You son of David!"

Those who led the way rebuked him, that he should be quiet; but he cried out all the more, "Lord, You son of David, have mercy on me!"

Jesus standing still, commanded and said, "Call him."

They called the blind man, saying to him, "Cheer up! Get up. He is calling you!"

He, casting away his cloak, sprang up, and came to Jesus. The crowd brought them both to Jesus.

When he had come near, He asked him, "What do you want Me to do for you?"

He said, "Lord, Rabboni, that I may see again." They both told Him, "Lord, that our eyes may be opened."

Jesus, being moved with compassion, touched their eyes; then Jesus said to them, "Receive your sight. Your faith has healed you."

Immediately they received their sight, and followed Him, glorifying God. All the people, when they saw it, praised God.

THE SALVATION OF ZACCHAEUS
Luke 19:1-10

He entered and was passing through Jericho. There was a man named Zacchaeus. He was a chief tax collector, and he was rich. He was trying to see who Jesus was, and couldn't because of the crowd, because he was short. He ran on ahead, and climbed up into a sycamore tree to see Him, for He was to pass that way.

When Jesus came to the place, He looked up and saw him, and said to him, "Zacchaeus, hurry and come down, for today I must stay at your house." He hurried, came down, and received Him joyfully.

When they saw it, they all murmured, saying, "He has gone in to lodge with a man who is a sinner."

Zacchaeus stood and said to the Lord, "Behold, Lord, half of my goods I give to the poor. If I have wrongfully exacted anything of anyone, I restore four times as much."

Jesus said to him, "Today, salvation has come to this house, because he also is a son of Abraham. For the Son of Man came to seek and to save that which was lost."

PARABLE OF THE TEN MINAS
Luke 19:11-28

As they heard these things, He went on and told a parable, because He was near Jerusalem, and they supposed that the Kingdom of God would be revealed immediately. He said therefore, "A certain nobleman went into a far country to receive for himself a kingdom, and to return. He called ten servants of his, and gave them ten mina coins, and told them, 'Conduct business until I come.'

"But his citizens hated him, and sent an envoy after him, saying, 'We don't want this man to reign over us.'

"It happened when he had come back again, having received the kingdom, that he commanded these servants, to whom he had given the money, to be called to him, that he might know what they had gained by conducting business.

"The first came before him, saying, 'Lord, your mina has made ten more minas.'

"He said to him, 'Well done, you good servant! Because you were found faithful in a very little, you shall have authority over ten cities.'

"The second came, saying, 'Your mina, lord, has made five minas.'

"So he said to him, 'And you are to be over five cities.'

"Another came, saying, 'Lord, behold, your mina, which I kept laid away in a handkerchief, for I feared you, because you are an exacting man. You take up that which you didn't lay down, and reap that which you didn't sow.'

"He said to him, 'Out of your own mouth will I judge you, you wicked servant! You knew that I am an exacting man, taking up that which I didn't lay down, and reaping that which I didn't sow. Then why didn't you deposit my money in the bank, and at my coming, I might have earned interest on it?'

"He said to those who stood by, 'Take the mina away from him, and give it to him who has the ten minas.'

"They said to him, 'Lord, he has ten minas!'

"He replied, 'For I tell you that to everyone who has, will more be given; but from him who doesn't have, even that which he has will be taken away from him.

But bring those enemies of mine who didn't want me to reign over them here, and kill them before me.'"

Having said these things, He went on ahead, going up to Jerusalem.

ARRIVAL AT BETHANY
John 11:55-12:1

Now the Passover of the Jews was at hand. Many went up from the country to Jerusalem before the Passover, to purify themselves. Then they sought for Jesus and spoke one with another, as they stood in the temple, "What do you think -- that He isn't coming to the feast at all?" Now the Chief Priests and the Pharisees had commanded that if anyone knew where He was, he should report it, that they might seize Him.

Then six days before the Passover, Jesus came to Bethany, where Lazarus was, who had been dead, whom He raised from the dead.

MARY ANOINTS JESUS' FEET
Matthew 26:6-13; Mark 14:3-9; John 12:2-11

Now when Jesus was in Bethany, in the house of Simon the leper, they made for Him a supper there. Martha served, and Lazarus was one of those who sat at the table with Him. As He sat at the table, Mary came having an alabaster jar of very expensive ointment of pure nard -- very costly and very precious. She broke the jar, and poured it over His head. She then took a pound of ointment of pure nard, and anointed the feet of Jesus, and wiped His feet with her hair. The house was filled with the fragrance of the ointment.

But when His disciples saw this, some were indignant, saying, "Why this waste? For this ointment might have been sold for much, and given to the poor" and "Why has this ointment been wasted?" They grumbled against her.

Then Judas Iscariot, Simon's son, one of His disciples, who would betray Him, said, "Why wasn't this ointment sold for three hundred denarii, and given to the poor?" Now he said this, not because he cared for the poor, but because he was a thief, and having the money box, used to steal what was put into it.

But Jesus, knowing this, said to them, "Why do you trouble the woman? Leave her alone. Because she has done a good work for Me. She has kept this for the day of My burial. For in pouring this ointment on My body, she did it to pre-pare Me for burial. For you always have the poor with you; and whenever you want to, you can do them good; but you don't always have Me. Most assuredly I tell you, wherever this gospel is preached in the whole world, what this woman has done will also be spoken of as a memorial of her."

A large crowd therefore of the Jews learned that He was there, and they came, not for Jesus' sake only, but that they might see Lazarus also, whom He had raised from the dead.

114

But the Chief Priests conspired to put Lazarus to death also, because on account of him many of the Jews went away and believed in Jesus.

TRIUMPHAL ENTRY INTO JERUSALEM
Matthew 21:1-11; Mark 11:1-11; Luke 19:29-44; John 12:12-19

On the next day a great multitude had come to the feast. It happened, when He drew near to Jerusalem, and came to Bethsphage and Bethany, at the mountain that is called Olivet, He sent two of His disciples, saying, "Go your way into the village on the other side, in which, as you enter, you will find a donkey tied, and a colt tied with her whereon no man ever yet sat. Untie them, and bring them to Me. If anyone asks you, 'Why are you untying it?' or 'Why are you doing this?', say to him: 'The Lord needs them,' and immediately he will send them."

All this was done, that it might be fulfilled which was spoken through the prophet, saying,

> "Tell the daughter of Zion,
>   don't be afraid, daughter of Zion.
> Behold, your King comes to you, humble, and riding on a donkey,
>   on a colt, the foal of a donkey."

His disciples didn't understand these things at first, but when Jesus was glorified, then they remembered that these things were written about Him, and that they had done these things to Him.

Those who were sent went away and did just as Jesus commanded them, and found things just as He had told them. They found a young donkey tied at the door outside in the open street, and they untied him. As they were untying the colt, the owners of it said to them, "What are you doing? Why are you untying the colt?"

They said to them just as Jesus had said, "The Lord needs it" and they let them go.

They brought the donkey and the colt to Jesus. They threw their cloaks on the colt, and set Jesus on them. As He went, they spread their cloaks in the way. As He was now getting near, at the descent of the Mount of Olives, a very great multitude, when they heard that Jesus was coming to Jerusalem, spread their clothes on the road. Others cut palm branches from the trees, and spread them on the road and went out to meet Him. The multitude therefore that was with Him when He called Lazarus out of the tomb, and raised him from the dead, was testifying about it. For this cause also the multitude went and met Him, because they heard that He had done this sign.

The whole multitude of the disciples began to rejoice and praise God with a loud voice for all the mighty works which they had seen, saying,

> "Hosanna to the son of David!

115

"Hosanna! Blessed is He Who comes in the name of the Lord,
   the King of Israel!
"Blessed is the Kingdom of our father David that is coming in
   the name of the Lord!
"Blessed is the King Who comes in the name of the Lord!
"Peace in Heaven, and glory in the highest!
"Hosanna in the highest!"

When He had come into Jerusalem, all the city was stirred up, saying, "Who is this?" The multitudes said, "This is the prophet, Jesus, from Nazareth of Galilee."

Some of the Pharisees from the multitude said to Him, "Teacher, rebuke Your disciples!"

He answered them, "I tell you that if these were silent, the stones would cry out."

The Pharisees therefore said among themselves, "See how you accomplish nothing. Behold, the world has gone after Him."

Jesus entered into the temple in Jerusalem. When He had looked around at everything, it being now evening, He went out to Bethany with the twelve. Before He left the temple, the blind and the lame came to Him, and He healed them.

But when the Chief Priests and the Scribes saw the wonderful things that He did, and the children who were crying in the temple and saying, "Hosanna to the son of David!" they were indignant, and said to Him, "Do You hear what these are saying?"

Jesus said to them, "Yes. Did you never read,

'Out of the mouth of babes and nursing babies you have perfected
   praise?'"

He left them, and went out of the city to Bethany, and lodged there. As He was leaving Jerusalem, He saw the city and wept over it, saying, "If you, even you, had known today the things which belong to your peace! But now, they are hidden from your eyes. For the days will come on you, when your enemies will throw up a barricade against you, surround you, hem you in on every side, and will dash you and your children within you to the ground. They will not leave in you one stone on another, because you didn't know the time of your visitation."

THE CURSING OF THE FIG TREE
Matthew 21:18-19a; Mark 11:12-14

The next day, in the morning, when they had come out from Bethany, as He returned to the city, He was hungry. Seeing a fig tree afar off having leaves, by the road, He came to it to see if perhaps He might find anything on it, and found nothing on it but leaves for it was not the season for figs. He said to it, "May no one ever eat fruit from you again! Let there be no fruit from you forever!"

THE SECOND CLEANSING OF THE TEMPLE
Matthew 21:12-13; Mark 11:15-18; Luke 19:45-48

When they came to Jerusalem, He entered into the temple of God, and began to drive out those who bought and sold in it, and overthrew the money-changers' tables and the seats of those who sold the doves. Also, He would not allow anyone to carry a container through the temple.

He taught, saying to them, "It is written,

'My house is a house of prayer for all the nations,
but you have made it a den of robbers!'"

But the Chief Priests and the Scribes and the leading men among the people, when they heard it, sought to destroy Him. He was teaching daily in the temple but they couldn't find a way to kill Him, for all the people hung on to every word that He said. For they feared Him, because all the multitude was astonished at His teaching.

Yet the Chief Priests and the Scribes continually sought how they might destroy Him.

JESUS AGAIN PREDICTS HIS DEATH
John 12:20-36

Now there were certain Greeks among those that went up to worship at the feast. These, therefore, came to Philip, who was from Bethsaida of Galilee, and asked him, saying, "Sir, we want to see Jesus." Philip came and told Andrew, and in turn, Andrew came with Philip, and they told Jesus.

Jesus answered them, "The time has come for the Son of Man to be glorified. Most assuredly I tell you, unless a grain of wheat falls into the earth and dies, it remains by itself alone. But if it dies, it bears much fruit. He who loves his life will lose it. He who hates his life in this world will keep it to eternal life. If anyone serves Me, let him follow Me. Where I am, there will My servant also be. If anyone serves Me, the Father will honor him.

"Now My soul is troubled. What shall I say? 'Father, save Me from this time?' But for this cause I came to this time. Father, glorify Your name!"

Then there came a voice out of the Heaven, saying, "I have both glorified it, and will glorify it again." The multitude therefore, who stood by and heard it, said that it had thundered. Others said, "An angel has spoken to Him."

Jesus answered, "This voice hasn't come for My sake, but for your sakes. Now is the judgment of this world. Now the prince of this world will be cast out. And I, if I am lifted up from the earth, will draw all people to Myself." But He said this, signifying by what kind of death He should die.

The multitude answered Him, "We have heard out of the law that the Christ remains forever. How do You say, 'The Son of Man must be lifted up?' Who is this Son of Man?"

Jesus therefore said to them, "Yet a little while the light is with you. Walk while you have the light, that darkness doesn't overtake you. He who walks in the darkness doesn't know where he is going. While you have the light, believe in the light, that you may become children of light."

Jesus said these things, and He departed and hid Himself from them.

CONTINUED UNBELIEF BY THE JEWS
John 12:37-50

But though He had done so many signs before them, yet they didn't believe in Him, that the word of Isaiah the prophet might be fulfilled, which he spoke,

> "Lord, who has believed our report?
> To whom has the arm of the Lord been revealed?"

For this cause they couldn't believe, for Isaiah said again,

> "He has blinded their eyes and He hardened their heart,
> lest they should see with their eyes, and perceive with their
> heart, and would turn, and I would heal them."

Isaiah said these things when he saw His glory, and spoke of Him.

Nevertheless even of the rulers many believed in Him, but because of the Pharisees they didn't confess it, so that they wouldn't be put out of the synagogue, for they loved men's praise more than God's praise.

Jesus cried out and said, "Whoever believes in Me, believes not in Me, but in Him Who sent Me. He who sees Me sees Him Who sent Me. I have come as a light into the world, that whoever believes in Me may not remain in the darkness.

"If anyone listens to My sayings, and doesn't believe, I don't judge him. For I came not to judge the world, but to save the world. He who rejects Me, and doesn't receive My sayings, has one who judges him. The word that I spoke, the same will judge him in the last day. For I spoke not from Myself, but the Father Who sent Me, He gave Me a commandment, what I should say, and what I should speak. I know that His commandment is eternal life. The things therefore which I speak, even as the Father has said to Me, so I speak."

THE WITHERED FIG TREE AND FAITH
Matthew 21:19b-22; Mark 11:19-26

When evening came, He went out of the city. As they passed by the next morning, they saw the fig tree withered away from the roots.

When the disciples saw it, they marveled, saying, "How did the fig tree immediately wither away?"

Peter, remembering, said to Him, "Rabbi, look! The fig tree which You cursed has withered away."

Jesus answered them, "Have faith in God. Most assuredly I tell you, if you have faith, and don't doubt, you will not only do what is done to the fig tree, but even if you told this mountain, 'Be taken up and cast into the sea,' and doesn't doubt in his heart, but believes that what he says is happening; it would be done for him and he shall have whatever he says.

"All things, whatever you ask in prayer, believing, you will receive. Therefore I tell you, all things whatever you pray and ask for, believe that you receive them, and you shall have them. Whenever you stand praying, forgive, if you have anything against anyone; so that your Father, Who is in Heaven, may also forgive you your transgressions. But if you do not forgive, neither will your Father in Heaven forgive your transgressions."

THE AUTHORITY OF JESUS IS QUESTIONED
Matthew 21:23-27; Mark 11:27-33; Luke 20:1-8

They came again to Jerusalem and it happened on one of those days, when He had come into the temple, as He was teaching the people in the temple and preaching the gospel, that the Chief Priests and Scribes came to Him with the Elders of the people. They asked Him, "Tell us: by what authority do You do these things? Or who is giving You this authority?"

He answered them, "I also will ask you one question, which if you tell Me, I likewise will tell you by what authority I do these things. The baptism of John, where was it from, was it from Heaven, or from men? Answer Me."

They reasoned with themselves, saying, "If we say, 'From Heaven,' He will say, 'Why didn't you believe him?' But if we say, 'From men,' we fear the multitude, all the people will stone us, for they are persuaded that John was really a prophet."

They answered that they didn't know where it was from.

Jesus said to them, "Neither will I tell you by what authority I do these things."

THE PARABLE OF THE TWO SONS
Matthew 21:28-32

"But what do you think? A man had two sons, and he came to the first, and said, 'Son, go work today in my vineyard.'

"He answered, 'I will not,' but afterward he changed his mind, and went.

"He came to the second, and said the same thing.

"He answered, 'I go, sir,' but he didn't go.

"Which of the two did the will of his father?"

They said to Him, "The first."

Jesus said to them, "Most assuredly I tell you that the tax collectors and the prostitutes are entering into the Kingdom of God before you. For John came to you in the way of righteousness, and you didn't believe him, but the tax collectors and the prostitutes believed him. When you saw it, you didn't even repent afterward, that you might believe him."

THE PARABLE OF THE TENANTS
Matthew 21:33-46; Mark 12:1-12; Luke 20:9-19

He began to tell the people this parable. "Hear another parable. There was a man who was a master of a household, who planted a vineyard, set a hedge about it, dug a pit for the winepress in it, built a tower, and rented it out to some farmers, and went into another country for a long time.

"At the proper season, when the season for the fruit drew near, he sent a servant to the farmers to collect his share of the fruit of the vineyard. But the farmers beat him, and sent him away empty. He sent yet another servant, and they also beat him, and treated him shamefully, and sent him away empty. He sent yet a third, and they also wounded him, and threw him out. Again, he sent other servants more than the first: and they treated them the same way. Again, he sent another servant to them; and they threw stones at him, wounded him in the head, and sent him away shamefully treated. Again he sent another; and they killed him; and many others, beating some, and killing some.

"The lord of the vineyard said, 'What shall I do? I will send my beloved son. It may be that seeing him, they will respect him.'

"But when the farmers saw him, they reasoned among themselves, saying, 'This is the heir. Come, let's kill him, that the inheritance may be ours.' They threw him out of the vineyard, and killed him.

"When therefore the lord of the vineyard comes, what will he do to them?"

They told him, "He will miserably destroy those miserable men, and will lease out the vineyard to other farmers, who will give him the fruit in its season. He will come and destroy these farmers, and will give the vineyard to others."

When they heard it, they said, "May it never be!"

But He looked at them, and said, "Did you never read in the Scriptures, what is this that is written,

> 'The stone which the builders rejected,
> the same was made the chief cornerstone?
> This was from the Lord. It is marvelous in Our eyes?

120

Everyone who falls on that stone will be broken to pieces,
but it will crush whomever it falls on to dust?'

"Therefore I tell you, the Kingdom of God will be taken away from you, and will be given to a nation bringing forth its fruits."

When the Chief Priests , the Pharisees, and the Scribes heard His parables, they perceived that He spoke the parable about them. They sought to lay hands on Him that very hour, but they feared the people because they considered Him to be a prophet and they knew He had spoken this parable against them. They left Him, and went away.

THE PARABLE OF THE WEDDING BANQUET
Matthew 22:1-14

Jesus answered and spoke again in parables to them, saying, "The Kingdom of Heaven is like a certain king, who made a marriage feast for his son, and sent out his servants to call those who were invited to the marriage feast, but they would not come.

"Again he sent out other servants, saying, 'Tell those who are invited, "Behold, I have made ready my dinner. My oxen and my fatlings are killed, and all things are ready. Come to the marriage feast!"'

"But they made light of it, and went their ways, one to his own farm, another to his merchandise, and the rest grabbed his servants, and treated them shamefully, and killed them. When the king heard that, he was angry, and he sent his armies, destroyed those murderers, and burned their city.

"Then he said to his servants, 'The wedding is ready, but those who were invited weren't worthy. Go therefore to the intersections of the highways, and as many as you may find, invite to the marriage feast.' Those servants went out into the highways, and gathered together as many as they found, both bad and good. The wedding was filled with guests.

"But when the king came in to see the guests, he saw there a man who didn't have on wedding clothing, and he said to him, 'Friend, how did you come in here not wearing wedding clothing?' He was speechless.

"Then the king said to the servants, 'Bind him hand and foot, take him away, and throw him into the outer darkness; there is where the weeping and grinding of teeth will be.'

"For many are called, but few chosen."

PAYING TAXES TO CAESAR
Matthew 22:15-22; Mark 12:13-17; Luke 20:20-26

Then the Pharisees went and took counsel how they might entrap Him in His talk. They watched Him, and sent out spies, their disciples, along with the Herodians, who pretended to be righteous, that they might trap Him in something He said, so as to deliver Him up to the power and authority of the governor. They asked Him, "Teacher, we know that You are honest, and don't defer to anyone; You say and teach what is right, and aren't partial to anyone, but truly teach the way of God in truth. Tell us therefore, what do You think? Is it lawful for us to pay taxes to Caesar, or not? Shall we give, or shall we not give?"

But He perceived their craftiness, hypocrisy, and wickedness, and said to them, "Why do you test Me you hypocrites? Show Me the tax money, show Me a denarius that I may see it."

They brought to Him a denarius.

"Whose image and inscription are on it?" He asked them.

They answered, "Caesar's."

He said to them, "Then give to Caesar the things that are Caesar's, and to God the things that are God's."

They weren't able to trap Him in His words before the people. They marveled greatly at His answer, and were silent and left Him, and went away.

SADDUCEES QUESTION JESUS
Matthew 22:23-33; Mark 12:18-27; Luke 20:27-40

On that day some of the Sadducees came to Him, those who deny that there is a resurrection. They asked Him, "Teacher, Moses wrote to us that if a man's brother dies having a wife, and he is childless, his brother should take the wife, and raise up children for his brother. There were therefore seven brothers. The first took a wife, and died childless. The second took her as wife, and he died childless. The third took her, and likewise the seven all left no children, and died. Afterward the woman also died. Therefore in the resurrection, when they rise, whose wife of them will she be? For the seven had her as a wife."

Jesus said to them, "You are mistaken, not knowing the Scriptures, nor the power of God. The children of this age marry, and are given in marriage. But those who are considered worthy to attain to that age and the resurrection from the dead, neither marry, nor are given in marriage but are like God's angels in Heaven. For they can't die any more, for they are like the angels, and are children of God, being children of the resurrection. But concerning the resurrection of the dead, that the dead are raised, haven't you read in the book of Moses, that which was spoken to you by God, even Moses showed at the bush, when he called the Lord 'The God of Abraham, the God of Isaac, and the God of Jacob'? Now He is not the God of the dead, but of the living, for all are alive to Him. You are therefore badly mistaken."

Some of the Scribes answered, "Teacher, You speak well." They didn't dare to ask Him any more questions.

When the multitudes heard it, they were astonished at His teaching.

THE GREATEST COMMANDMENT
Matthew 22:34-40; Mark 12:28-34

But the Pharisees, when they heard that He had put the Sadducees to silence, gathered themselves together. One of them, a Lawyer or Scribe, had heard them questioning Jesus and knowing that He had answered them well, asked Him a question, testing Him. "Teacher, which is the greatest commandment in the law? Which commandment is the greatest of all?"

Jesus said to him, "The greatest is, 'Hear, Israel, the Lord our God, the Lord is one: You shall love the Lord your God with all your heart, and with all your soul, and with all your mind, and with all your strength.' This is the first and great commandment. A second likewise is this, 'You shall love your neighbor as yourself.' There is no other commandment greater than these. The whole law and the prophets depend on these two commandments."

The Scribe said to Him, "Truly, teacher, You have said well that He is one, and there is none other but He, and to love Him with all the heart, and with all the understanding, with all the soul, and with all the strength, and to love his neighbor as himself, is more important than all whole burnt offerings and sacrifices."

When Jesus saw that he answered wisely, He said to him, "You are not far from the Kingdom of God."

No one dared ask Him any question after that.

WHOSE SON IS CHRIST?
Matthew 22:41-46; Mark 12:35-37; Luke 20:41-44

Now while the Pharisees were gathered together, Jesus asked them a question, saying, "What do you think of the Christ? Whose son is He?"

They said to Him, "Of David."

He said to them, "Why do they say that the Christ is David's son? How then does David in the Holy Spirit call Him 'Lord', for David himself says in the book of Psalms,

'The Lord said to my Lord, "Sit at My right hand, until I make Your enemies the footstool of Your feet."'

"If then David therefore calls Him Lord, so how is He his son?"

No one was able to answer Him a word, neither dared any man from that day forth ask Him any more questions. The common people heard Him gladly.

WOES TO THE SCRIBES AND PHARISEES
Matthew 23:1-36; Mark 12:38-40; Luke 20:45-47

In the hearing of all the people, He said to His disciples, and to the multitudes, saying, "The Scribes and the Pharisees sat on Moses' seat. All things therefore

123

whatever they tell you to observe, observe and do, but don't do their works; for they say, and don't do. For they bind heavy burdens that are grievous to be borne, and lay them on men's shoulders; but they themselves will not lift a finger to help them.

"Beware of the Scribes, who like to walk in long robes, they make their phylacteries broad, enlarge the fringes of their garments, and love greetings in the marketplaces, the best seats in the synagogues, and the best places at feasts; who devour widows' houses, and for a pretense make long prayers: these will receive greater condemnation.

"But all their works they do to be seen by men, and love the place of honor at feasts, the best seats in the synagogues, the salutations in the marketplaces, and to be called 'Rabbi, Rabbi' by men.

"But don't you be called 'Rabbi,' for one is your teacher, the Christ, and all of you are brothers. Call no man on the earth your father, for one is your Father, He Who is in Heaven. Neither be called masters, for one is your Master, the Christ. But he who is greatest among you will be your servant. Whoever exalts himself will be humbled, and whoever humbles himself will be exalted.

"Woe to you, Scribes and Pharisees, hypocrites! For you devour widows' houses, and as a pretense you make long prayers. Therefore you will receive greater condemnation.

"But woe to you, Scribes and Pharisees, hypocrites! Because you shut up the Kingdom of Heaven against men; for you don't enter in yourselves, neither do you allow those who are entering in to enter.

"Woe to you, Scribes and Pharisees, hypocrites! For you travel around by sea and land to make one proselyte; and when he becomes one, you make him twice as much of a son of Gehenna as yourselves.

"Woe to you, you blind guides, who say, 'Whoever swears by the temple, it is nothing; but whoever swears by the gold of the temple, he is obligated.' You blind fools! For which is greater, the gold, or the temple that sanctifies the gold? 'Whoever swears by the altar, it is nothing; but whoever swears by the gift that is on it, he is obligated.' You blind fools! For which is greater, the gift, or the altar that sanctifies the gift? He therefore who swears by the altar, swears by it, and by everything on it. He who swears by the temple, swears by it, and by Him Who was living in it. He who swears by Heaven, swears by the throne of God, and by Him Who sits on it.

"Woe to you, Scribes and Pharisees, hypocrites! For you tithe mint, dill, and cumin, and have left undone the weightier matters of the law: justice, mercy, and faith. But you ought to have done these, and not to have left the other undone. You blind guides, who strain out a gnat, and swallow a camel!

"Woe to you, Scribes and Pharisees, hypocrites! For you clean the outside of the cup and of the platter, but within they are full of extortion and unrighteousness.

You blind Pharisee, first clean the inside of the cup and of the platter, that the outside of it may become clean also.

"Woe to you, Scribes and Pharisees, hypocrites! For you are like whitened tombs, which outwardly appear beautiful, but inwardly are full of dead men's bones, and of all uncleanness. Even so you also outwardly appear righteous to men, but inwardly you are full of hypocrisy and iniquity.

"Woe to you, Scribes and Pharisees, hypocrites! For you build the tombs of the prophets, and decorate the tombs of the righteous, and say, 'If we had lived in the days of our fathers, we wouldn't have been partakers with them in the blood of the prophets.' Therefore you testify to yourselves that you are children of those who killed the prophets. Fill up, then, the measure of your fathers.

"You serpents, you offspring of vipers, how will you escape the judgment of Gehenna? Therefore, behold, I send to you prophets, wise men, and Scribes. Some of them you will kill and crucify; and some of them you will scourge in your synagogues, and persecute from city to city; that on you may come all the righteous blood shed on the earth, from the blood of righteous Abel to the blood of Zachariah son of Barachiah, whom you killed between the sanctuary and the altar. Most assuredly I tell you, all these things will come upon this generation.

LAMENT OVER JERUSALEM
Matthew 23:37-39

"Jerusalem, Jerusalem, who kills the prophets, and stones those who are sent to her! How often would I have gathered your children together, even as a hen gathers her chickens under her wings, and you would not! Behold, your house is left to you desolate. For I tell you, you will not see Me from now on, until you say, 'Blessed is He Who comes in the name of the Lord!'"

THE POOR WIDOW'S GIFT
Mark 12:41-44; Luke 21:1-4

Jesus sat down opposite the treasury, and saw how the multitude cast money into the treasury. Many who were rich cast in much. He looked up, and saw the rich people who were putting their gifts into the treasury. He saw a certain poor widow casting in two small brass coins, which equal a quadrans coin. He called His disciples to Himself, and said to them, "Truly I tell you, this poor widow put in more than all of them, for all these put in gifts for God from their abundance, but she, out of her poverty, put in all that she had to live on."

THE DESTRUCTION OF THE TEMPLE FORETOLD
THE DESTRUCTION OF JERUSALEM FORETOLD
THE SECOND COMING FORETOLD
Matthew 24:1-41; Mark 13:1-32; Luke 21:5-33

Jesus went out from the temple, and was going on His way and His disciples came to Him to show Him the buildings of the temple and some were talking about the temple and how it was decorated with beautiful stones and gifts, and one

125

of His disciples said to Him, "Teacher, see what kind of stones and what kind of buildings!" He said, "Do you see these great buildings? As for these things which you see, most assuredly I tell you, the days will come, in which there will not be left here one stone on another that will not be thrown down."

As He sat on the Mount of Olives opposite the temple, the disciples, Peter, James, John, and Andrew came to Him privately, and they asked Him, "Teacher, so when will these things be? What is the sign that these things are about to happen? What is the sign of Your coming, and of the end of the age?"

Jesus answered them, and He said, "Watch out that you don't get led astray, for many will come in My name, saying, 'I am the Christ,' 'I AM,' and, 'The time is at hand' and will lead many astray. Therefore don't follow them. Many false prophets will arise, and will lead many astray. When you hear of wars, rumors of wars, and disturbances, don't be terrified or troubled, for these things must happen first, but the end won't come immediately."

Then He said to them, "Nation will rise against nation, and kingdom against kingdom. There will be great earthquakes, famines, troubles, and plagues in various places. There will be terrors and great signs from Heaven. But all these things are the beginning of birth pains.

"But before all these things, then they will deliver you up to oppression, and will kill you. You will be hated by all of the nations for My name's sake. They will lay their hands on you and will persecute you, delivering you up to synagogues and prisons, bringing you before kings and governors for My name's sake for a testimony to them. You will be beaten in synagogues. It will turn out as a testimony for you. Settle it therefore in your hearts not to meditate beforehand how to answer, for I will give you a mouth and wisdom which all your adversaries will not be able to withstand or to contradict. You will be handed over even by parents, brothers, relatives, and friends. Some of you they will cause to be put to death. You will be hated by all men for My name's sake. Not a hair of your head will perish. Then many will stumble, and will deliver up one another, and will hate one another. Because iniquity will be multiplied, the love of many will grow cold. By your endurance you will win your lives and he who endures to the end, the same will be saved. This gospel of the Kingdom will be preached in the whole world for a testimony to all the nations, and then the end will come.

"But when you see Jerusalem surrounded by armies, then know that its desolation is at hand. When, therefore, you see the abomination of desolation, which was spoken of through Daniel the prophet, standing in the holy place, where it ought not, (let the reader understand), then let those who are in Judea flee to the mountains. Let him who is on the housetop not go down to take out things that are in his house. Let him who is in the field not return back to get his clothes. Pray that your flight will not be in the winter, nor on a Sabbath, and let those who are in the midst of her depart. Let those who are in the country not enter therein. For these are days of vengeance, that all things which are written may be fulfilled and there will be great oppression, such as has not been from the beginning of the world until now, no, nor ever will be. Unless those days had been shortened, no flesh would have been saved. But for the elect's sake, those days will be shortened. Woe to those who are pregnant and to those who nurse infants in those days! For there will be great distress in the land, and wrath to this people. They will fall by the edge of the sword, and will be led captive into all the nations. Jerusalem will be trampled down by the Gentiles, until the times of the Gentiles are fulfilled.

"Then if any man tells you, 'Behold, here is the Christ,' or, 'There,' don't believe it. For there will arise false christs, and false prophets, and they will show great signs and wonders, so as to lead astray, if possible, even the elect.

"But you watch. Behold, I have told you beforehand. If therefore they tell you, 'Behold, He is in the wilderness,' don't go out; 'Behold, He is in the inner chambers,' don't believe it. For as the lightning comes forth from the east, and is seen even to the west, so will be the coming of the Son of Man. For wherever the carcass is, there will the vultures be gathered together. But immediately after the oppression of those days, the sun will be darkened, the moon will not give its light, the stars will fall from heaven, and the powers of the heavens will be shaken; and then the sign of the Son of Man will appear in the heavens. Then all the tribes of the earth will mourn, and they will see the Son of Man coming on the clouds of heaven with power and great glory. He will send out His angels with a great sound of a trumpet, and they will gather together His elect from the four winds, from one end of heaven to the other.

"There will be signs in the sun, moon, and stars; and on the earth anxiety of nations, in perplexity for the roaring of the sea and the waves; men fainting for fear, and for expectation of the things which are coming on the world: for the powers of the heavens will be shaken. Then they will see the Son of Man coming in a cloud with power and great glory. But when these things begin to happen, look up, and lift up your heads, because your redemption is near."

He told them a parable. "See the fig tree, and all the trees and learn this parable. When its branch has now become tender, and puts forth its leaves, and when they are already budding, you see it and know by your own selves that the summer is already near. Even so you also, when you see these things happening, know that the Kingdom of God is near, even at the doors.

"Most assuredly I tell you, this generation will not pass away until all things are accomplished. Heaven and earth will pass away, but My words will by no means pass away.

"But of that day and hour, no one knows, not even the angels of Heaven, nor the Son, but My Father only. As the days of Noah were, so will be the coming of the Son of Man. For as in those days which were before the flood they were eating and drinking, marrying and giving in marriage, until the day that Noah entered into the ark, and they didn't know until the flood came, and took them all away, so will be the coming of the Son of Man. Then two men will be in the field: one will be taken and one will be left; two women grinding at the mill, one will be taken and one will be left.

PARABLES TEACHING WATCHFULNESS
Matthew 24:42-25:30; Mark 13:33-37; Luke 21:34-36

"So be careful, or your hearts will be loaded down with carousing, drunkenness, and cares of this life, and that day will come on you suddenly. For it will come like a snare on all those who dwell on the surface of all the earth. Watch, keep alert, and pray; for you don't know when the time is. Therefore be watchful all the time, asking that you may be counted worthy to escape all these things that will happen, and to stand before the Son of Man."

"It is like a man, traveling to another country, having left his house, and given authority to his servants, and to each one his work, and also commanded the door-keeper to keep watch. Watch therefore, for you don't know in what hour your lord of the house comes, whether at evening, or at midnight, or when the rooster crows, or in the morning; lest coming suddenly he might find you sleeping. But know this, that if the master of the house had known in what watch of the night the thief was coming, he would have watched, and would not have allowed his house to be broken into. Therefore also be ready, for in an hour that you don't expect, the Son of Man will come. What I tell you, I tell all: Watch."

"Who then is the faithful and wise servant, whom his lord has set over his household, to give them their food in due season? Blessed is that servant whom his lord finds doing so when he comes. Most assuredly I tell you that he will set him over all that he has. But if that evil servant should say in his heart, 'My lord is delaying his coming,' and begins to beat his fellow-servants, and eat and drink with the drunken, the lord of that servant will come in a day when he doesn't expect it, and in an hour when he doesn't know it, and will cut him in pieces, and appoint his portion with the hypocrites; there is where the weeping and grinding of teeth will be.

"Then the Kingdom of Heaven will be like ten virgins, who took their lamps, and went out to meet the bridegroom. Five of them were foolish, and five were wise. Those who were foolish, when they took their lamps, took no oil with them, but the wise took oil in their vessels with their lamps. Now while the bridegroom delayed, they all slumbered and slept.

"But at midnight there was a cry, 'Behold! The bridegroom is coming! Come out to meet him!'

"Then all those virgins arose, and trimmed their lamps. The foolish said to the wise, 'Give us some of your oil, for our lamps are going out.'

"But the wise answered, saying, 'What if there isn't enough for us and you? You go rather to those who sell, and buy for yourselves.'

"While they went away to buy, the bridegroom came, and those who were ready went in with him to the marriage feast, and the door was shut.

"Afterward the other virgins also came, saying, 'Lord, lord, open to us.'

"But he answered, 'Most assuredly I tell you, I don't know you.'

"Watch therefore, for you don't know the day nor the hour in which the Son of Man is coming.

"For it is like a man, going into another country, who called his own servants, and entrusted his goods to them. To one he gave five talents, to another two, to another one; to each according to his own ability. Then he went on his journey. Immediately he who received the five talents went and traded with them, and made another five talents. In like manner he also who got the two gained another two. But he who received the one went away and dug in the earth, and hid his lord's money.

"Now after a long time the lord of those servants came, and reconciled accounts with them. He who received the five talents came and brought another five talents, saying, 'Lord, you delivered to me five talents. Behold, I have gained another five talents besides them.'

"His lord said to him, 'Well done, good and faithful servant. You have been faithful over a few things, I will set you over many things. Enter into the joy of your lord.'

"He also who got the two talents came and said, 'Lord, you delivered to me two talents. Behold, I have gained another two talents besides them.'

"His lord said to him, 'Well done, good and faithful servant. You have been faithful over a few things, I will set you over many things. Enter into the joy of your lord.'

"He also who had received the one talent came and said, 'Lord, I knew you, that you are a hard man, reaping where you did not sow, and gathering where you did not scatter. I was afraid, and went away and hid your talent in the earth. Behold, you have what is yours.'

"But his lord answered him, 'You wicked and slothful servant. You knew that I reap where I didn't sow, and gather where I didn't scatter. You ought therefore to have deposited my money with the bankers, and at my coming I should have received back my own with interest. Take away therefore the talent from him, and give it to him who has the ten talents. For to everyone who has will be given, and he will have abundance, but from him who has not, even that which he has will be taken away. Throw out the unprofitable servant into the outer darkness, where there will be weeping and gnashing of teeth.'

THE JUDGMENT SEAT OF CHRIST
Matthew 25:31-46

"But when the Son of Man comes in His glory, and all the holy angels with Him, then He will sit on the throne of His glory. Before Him all the nations will be gathered, and He will separate them one from another, as a shepherd separates the sheep from the goats. He will set the sheep on His right hand, but the goats on the left.

"Then the King will tell those on His right hand, 'Come, blessed of My Father, inherit the Kingdom prepared for you from the foundation of the world; for I was hungry, and you gave Me food to eat; I was thirsty, and you gave Me drink; I was a stranger, and you took Me in; naked, and you clothed Me; I was sick, and you visited Me; I was in prison, and you came to Me.'

"Then the righteous will answer Him, saying, 'Lord, when did we see You hungry, and feed You; or thirsty, and give You a drink? When did we see You as a stranger, and take You in; or naked, and clothe You? When did we see You sick, or in prison, and come to You?'

"The King will answer them, 'Most assuredly I tell you, inasmuch as you did it to one of the least of these My brothers, you did it to Me.'

"Then He will say also to those on the left hand, 'Depart from Me, you cursed, into the eternal fire which is prepared for the devil and his angels; for I was hungry, and you didn't give Me food to eat; I was thirsty, and you gave Me no drink; I was a stranger, and you didn't take Me in; naked, and you didn't clothe Me; sick, and in prison, and you didn't visit Me.'

"Then they will also answer, saying, 'Lord, when did we see You hungry, or thirsty, or a stranger, or naked, or sick, or in prison, and didn't help You?'

"Then He will answer them, saying, 'Most assuredly I tell you, inasmuch as you didn't do it to one of the least of these, you didn't do it to Me.'

"These will go away into eternal punishment, but the righteous into eternal life."

THE PLOT AGAINST JESUS INTENSIFIES
Matthew 26:1-5; Mark 14:1-2; Luke 21:37-22:2

It happened, when Jesus had finished all these words, that He said to His disciples, "You know that after two days the Passover is coming, and the Son of Man will be delivered up to be crucified."

Now the feast of unleavened bread, which is called the Passover, drew near. It was now only two days before the feast of the Passover and the unleavened bread. Then the Chief Priests , the Scribes, and the Elders of the people were gathered together in the court of the high priest, who was called Caiaphas and they sought how they might seize Him by deception, and put Him to death. But they said, "Not during the feast, lest a riot occur among the people," for they feared the people.

Every day Jesus was teaching in the temple, and every night He would go out, and spent the night on the mountain that is called Olivet. All the people came early in the morning to Him in the temple to hear Him.

JUDAS AGREES TO BETRAY JESUS
Matthew 26:14-16; Mark 14:10-11; Luke 22:3-6

Satan entered into Judas, who was surnamed Iscariot, who was numbered with the twelve. He went away, and talked with the Chief Priests and captains about how he might deliver Him to them. He asked them, "What are you willing to give me, that I should deliver Him to you?" They were glad, and promised and agreed to give him money and they weighed out for him thirty pieces of silver. He consented, and sought an opportunity to betray and conveniently deliver Him to them in the absence of the multitude.

PREPARING THE PASSOVER MEAL
Matthew 26:17-19; Mark 14:12-16; Luke 22:7-13

Now on the first day of unleavened bread, on which the Passover must be sacrificed, He sent Peter and John, saying, "Go and prepare the Passover for us, that we may eat."

They asked Him, "Where do You want us to prepare for You to eat the Passover?"

He said to them, "Go into the city and behold, when you have entered into the city, a certain man carrying a pitcher of water will meet you. Follow him into the house which he enters. Tell the master of the house, 'The Teacher says to you, "My time is at hand. I will keep the Passover at your house with My disciples. Where is the guest room, where I may eat the Passover with My disciples?"' He will himself show you a large, furnished and ready upper room. Make preparations there."

They went out, and came into the city, and did as Jesus commanded them, and found all things as He had told them, and they prepared the Passover.

THE PASSOVER MEAL BEGINS
Matthew 26:20; Mark 14:17; Luke 22:14-16

Now when evening had come and when the hour had come, He sat down and He was reclining at the table with the twelve apostles. He said to them, "I have earnestly desired to eat this Passover with you before I suffer, for I tell you, I will no longer by any means eat of it until it is fulfilled in the Kingdom of God."

WASHING THE DISCIPLE'S FEET
John 13:1-20

Now before the feast of the Passover, Jesus knowing that His time had come that He would depart from this world to the Father, having loved His own who were in the world, He loved them to the end.

After supper, the devil having already put into the heart of Judas Iscariot, Simon's son, to betray Him, Jesus, knowing that the Father had given all things into His hands, and that He came forth from God, and was going to God, arose from supper, and laid aside His outer garments. He took a towel, and wrapped a towel around His waist. Then He poured water into the basin, and began to wash the disciples' feet, and to wipe them with the towel that was wrapped around Him.

Then He came to Simon Peter. He said to Him, "Lord, do You wash my feet?"

Jesus answered him, "You don't know what I am doing now, but you will understand later."

Peter said to Him, "You will never wash my feet!"

Jesus answered him, "If I don't wash you, you have no part with Me."

Simon Peter said to Him, "Lord, not my feet only, but also my hands and my head!"

Jesus said to him, "Someone who has bathed only needs to have his feet washed, but is completely clean. You are clean, but not all of you." For He knew him who would betray Him, therefore He said, "You are not all clean."

So when He had washed their feet, put His outer garment back on, and sat down again, He said to them, "Do you know what I have done to you? You call Me, 'Teacher' and 'Lord.' You say so correctly, for so I am. If I then, the Lord and the Teacher, have washed your feet, you also ought to wash one another's feet. For I have given you an example, that you also should do as I have done to you. Most assuredly I tell you, a servant is not greater than his lord, neither one who is sent greater than he who sent him. If you know these things, blessed are you if you do them.

"I don't speak concerning all of you. I know whom I have chosen. But that the Scripture may be fulfilled,

'He who eats bread with Me has lifted up his heel against Me.'

"From now on, I tell you before it happens, that when it happens, you may believe that I AM. Most assuredly I tell you, he who receives whomever I send, receives Me; and he who receives Me, receives Him Who sent Me."

THE BETRAYER IS IDENTIFIED
Matthew 26:21-25; Mark 14:18-21; Luke 22:21-23; John 13:21-30

When Jesus had said this, He was troubled in Spirit, **and** as they were eating, He said, "Most assuredly I tell you that one of you will betray Me -- He who eats with Me. Behold, the hand of him who betrays Me is with Me on the table.

They began to question among themselves, which of them it was who would do this thing. They were exceedingly sorrowful, and each began to ask Him one by one, "It isn't me, is it, Lord? Surely not I?"

He answered, "It is one of the twelve, he who dipped his hand with Me in the dish, the same will betray Me. The Son of Man indeed goes, as it has been determined, even as it is written of Him, but woe to that man through whom He, the Son of Man is betrayed! It would be better for that man if he had not been born."

The disciples looked at one another, perplexed about whom He spoke. One of His disciples, whom Jesus loved, was at the table, leaning against Jesus' breast. He, leaning back, as he was, on Jesus' breast, asked Him, "Lord, who is it?"

Jesus therefore answered, "It is he to whom I will give this piece of bread when I have dipped it." So when He had dipped the piece of bread, He gave it to Judas, the son of Simon Iscariot. Simon Peter therefore beckoned to him, and said to him, "Tell us who it is of whom He speaks."

Judas, who betrayed Him, answered, "It isn't me, is it, Rabbi?"

He said to him, "You said it."

After the piece of bread, then Satan entered into him. Then Jesus said to him, "What you do, do quickly."

Now no man at the table knew why He said this to him. For some thought, because Judas had the money box, that Jesus said to him, "Buy what things we need for the feast," or that he should give something to the poor. Therefore, having received that morsel, he went out immediately. It was night.

ARGUMENTS ABOUT GREATNESS
Luke 22:24-30

There arose also a contention among them, which of them was considered to be greatest.

He said to them, "The kings of the Gentiles lord it over them, and those who have authority over them are called 'benefactors.' But not so with you. But one who is the greater among you, let him become as the younger, and one who is governing, as one who serves. For who is greater, one who sits at the table, or one who serves? Isn't it he who sits at the table? But I am in the midst of you as one who serves. But you are those who have continued with Me in My trials. I confer on you a Kingdom, even as My Father conferred on Me, that you may eat and drink at My table in My Kingdom. You will sit on thrones, judging the twelve tribes of Israel."

THE FIRST PREDICTION OF PETER'S DENIAL
Luke 22:31-38; John 13:31-38

When he, (Judas), had gone out, Jesus said, "Now the Son of Man has been glorified, and God has been glorified in Him. If God has been glorified in Him, God will also glorify Him in Himself, and He will glorify Him immediately. Little children, I will be with you a little while longer. You will seek Me, and as I said to the Jews, 'Where I am going, you can't come,' so now I tell you. A new com-

133

mandment I give to you, that you love one another, just like I have loved you; that you also love one another. By this everyone will know that you are My disciples, if you have love for one another."

Simon Peter said to Him, "Lord, where are You going?"

Jesus answered, "Where I am going, you can't follow now, but you will follow afterwards."

Peter said to Him, "Lord, why can't I follow You now? I will lay down my life for you."

Jesus answered him, "Will you lay down your life for Me? Most assuredly I tell you, the rooster won't crow **twice** until you have denied Me three times.

The Lord said, "Simon, Simon, behold, Satan asked to have you, that he might sift you as wheat, but I prayed for you, that your faith wouldn't fail. You, when once you have turned again, establish your brothers."

He said to Him, "Lord, I am ready to go with You both to prison and to death!"

He said, "I tell you, Peter, the rooster will by no means crow twice today until you deny that you know Me three times." He said to them, "When I sent you out without purse, and wallet, and shoes, did you lack anything?"

They said, "Nothing."

Then He said to them, "But now, whoever has a purse, let him take it, and likewise a wallet. Whoever has none, let him sell his cloak, and buy a sword. For I tell you that this which is written must still be fulfilled in Me:

'He was counted with the lawless.'

For that which concerns Me has an end."

They said, "Lord, behold, here are two swords."

He said to them, "That is enough."

THE LORD'S SUPPER IS INSTITUTED
Matthew 26:26-29; Mark 14:22-25; Luke 22:17-20

He received a cup, and when He had given thanks, He said, "Take this, and share it among yourselves, for I tell you, I will not drink at all again from the fruit of the vine, until the Kingdom of God comes."

As they were eating, He took bread, and when He had given thanks, He broke it, and gave to them, saying, "Take, eat; this is My body which is given for you. Do this in memory of Me."

Likewise, He took the cup after supper, gave thanks, and gave it to them, saying, "All of you drink it, this cup is the new covenant in My blood, which is poured out for you and for many for the remission of sins." They all drank of it.

"Most assuredly I tell you that I will not drink of this fruit of the vine from now on, until that day when I drink it anew with you in My Father's Kingdom and Kingdom of God."

JESUS COMFORTS THE DISCIPLES
AND PROMISES THE HOLY SPIRIT
John 14:1-31

"Don't let your heart be troubled. Believe in God. Believe also in Me. In My Father's house are many mansions. If it weren't so, I would have told you. I am going to prepare a place for you. If I go and prepare a place for you, I will come again, and will receive you to Myself; that where I am, you may be there also. Where I go, you know, and you know the way."

Thomas says to Him, "Lord, we don't know where You are going. How can we know the way?"

Jesus said to him, "I am the way, the truth, and the life. No one comes to the Father, except through Me. If you had known Me, you would have known My Father also. From now on, you know Him, and have seen Him."

Philip said to Him, "Lord, show us the Father, and that will be enough for us."

Jesus said to him, "Have I been with you such a long time, and do you not know Me, Philip? He who has seen Me has seen the Father. How do you say, 'Show us the Father?' Don't you believe that I am in the Father, and the Father in Me? The words that I tell you, I speak not from Myself; but the Father Who lives in Me does His works. Believe Me that I am in the Father, and the Father in Me; or else believe Me for the very works' sake. Most assuredly I tell you, he who believes in Me, the works that I do, he will do also; and greater works than these will he do; because I am going to My Father. Whatever you will ask in My name, that will I do, that the Father may be glorified in the Son. If you will ask anything in My name, I will do it.

"If you love Me, keep My commandments. I will pray to the Father, and He will give you another Counselor, that He may be with you forever, -- the Spirit of truth, Whom the world can't receive; for it doesn't see Him, neither knows Him. You know Him, for He lives with you, and will be in you. I will not leave you orphans. I will come to you. Yet a little while, and the world will see Me no more; but you will see Me. Because I live, you will live also. In that day you will know that I am in My Father, and you in Me, and I in you. One who has My commandments, and keeps them, that person is one who loves Me. One who loves Me will be loved by My Father, and I will love him, and will reveal Myself to him."

Judas (not Iscariot) said to Him, "Lord, what has happened that You are about to reveal Yourself to us, and not to the world?"

Jesus answered him, "If a man loves Me, he will keep My word. My Father will love him, and We will come to him, and make Our home with him. He who doesn't love Me doesn't keep My words. The word which you hear isn't Mine, but the Father's Who sent Me.

"I have said these things to you, while still living with you. But the Counselor, the Holy Spirit, Whom the Father will send in My name, He will teach you all things, and will remind you of all that I said to you. Peace I leave with you. My peace I give to you; not as the world gives, give I to you. Don't let your heart be troubled, neither let it be fearful.

"You heard how I told you, 'I go away, and I come to you.' If you loved Me, you would have rejoiced, because I said 'I am going to My Father;' for the Father is greater than I. Now I have told you before it happens so that, when it happens, you may believe. I will no more speak much with you, for the prince of the world comes, and he has nothing in Me. But that the world may know that I love the Father, and as the Father commanded Me, even so I do.

"Arise, let us go from here."

THE VINE AND THE BRANCHES
John 15:1-17

"I am the true vine, and My Father is the farmer. Every branch in Me that doesn't bear fruit, He takes away. Every branch that bears fruit, He prunes, that it may bear more fruit. You are already pruned clean because of the word which I have spoken to you. Remain in Me, and I in you. As the branch can't bear fruit by itself, unless it remains in the vine, so neither can you, unless you remain in Me.

"I am the vine. You are the branches. He who remains in Me, and I in him, the same bears much fruit, for apart from Me you can do nothing. If a man doesn't remain in Me, he is thrown out as a branch, and is withered; and they gather them, throw them into the fire, and they are burned. If you remain in Me, and My words remain in you, you will ask whatever you desire, and it will be done for you. In this is My Father glorified, that you bear much fruit; and so you will be My disciples.

"Even as the Father has loved Me, I also have loved you. Remain in My love. If you keep My commandments, you will remain in My love; even as I have kept My Father's commandments, and remain in His love. I have spoken these things to you, that My joy may remain in you, and that your joy may be made full. This is My commandment, that you love one another, even as I have loved you. Greater love has no one than this, that someone lay down his life for his friends. You are My friends, if you do whatever I command you. No longer do I call you servants, for the servant doesn't know what his lord does. But I have called you friends, for everything that I heard from My Father, I have made known to you. You didn't choose Me, but I chose you, and appointed you, that you should go and bear fruit, and that your fruit should remain; that whatever you will ask of the Father in My name, He may give it to you. I command these things to you, that you may love one another.

OPPOSITION FROM THE WORLD
John 15:18-16:4

"If the world hates you, you know that it has hated Me before it hated you. If you were of the world, the world would love its own. But because you are not of the world, since I chose you out of the world, therefore the world hates you. Remember the word that I said to you: 'A servant is not greater than his lord.' If they persecuted Me, they will also persecute you. If they kept My word, they will keep yours also. But all these things will they do to you for My name's sake, because they don't know Him Who sent Me. If I had not come and spoken to them, they would not have had sin; but now they have no excuse for their sin. He who hates Me, hates My Father also. If I hadn't done among them the works which no one else did, they wouldn't have had sin. But now have they seen and also hated both Me and My Father. But this happened so that the word may be fulfilled which was written in their law,

'They hated Me without a cause.'

"When the Counselor has come, Whom I will send to you from the Father, the Spirit of truth, Who proceeds from the Father, He will testify about Me. You will also testify, because you have been with Me from the beginning.

"These things have I spoken to you, so that you wouldn't be caused to stumble. They will put you out of the synagogues. Yes, the time comes that whoever kills you will think that he offers service to God. They will do these things because they have not known the Father, nor Me. But I have told you these things, so that when the time comes, you may remember that I told you about them. I didn't tell you these things from the beginning, because I was with you.

THE WORK OF THE HOLY SPIRIT
John 16:5-15

"But now I am going to Him Who sent Me, and none of you asks Me, 'Where are You going?' But because I have told you these things, sorrow has filled your heart. Nevertheless I tell you the truth: It is to your advantage that I go away, for if I don't go away, the Counselor won't come to you. But if I go, I will send Him to you. When He has come, He will convict the world about sin, about righteousness, and about judgment; about sin, because they don't believe in Me; about righteousness, because I am going to My Father, and you won't see Me any more; about judgment, because the prince of this world has been judged.

"I have yet many things to tell you, but you can't bear them now. However when He, the Spirit of truth, has come, He will guide you into all truth, for He will not speak from Himself; but whatever He hears, He will speak. He will declare to you things that are coming. He will glorify Me, for He will take from what is Mine, and will declare it to you. All things whatever the Father has are Mine; therefore I said that He takes of Mine, and will declare it to you.

GRIEF OF THE DISCIPLES WILL BE TURNED INTO JOY
John 16:16-22

"A little while, and you will not see Me. Again a little while, and you will see Me."

Some of His disciples therefore said to one another, "What is this that He says to us, 'A little while, and you won't see Me, and again a little while, and you will see Me;' and, 'Because I go to the Father?'" They said therefore, "What is this that He says, 'A little while?' We don't know what He is saying."

Therefore Jesus perceived that they wanted to ask Him, and He said to them, "Do you inquire among yourselves concerning this, that I said, 'A little while, and you won't see Me, and again a little while, and you will see Me?' Most assuredly I tell you, that you will weep and lament, but the world will rejoice. You will be sorrowful, but your sorrow will be turned into joy. A woman, when she gives birth, has sorrow, because her time has come. But when she has delivered the child, she doesn't remember the anguish any more, for the joy that a human being is born into the world. Therefore you now have sorrow, but I will see you again, and your heart will rejoice, and no one will take your joy away from you.

PROMISE OF PEACE
John 16:23-33

"In that day you will ask Me no questions. Most assuredly I tell you, whatever you may ask of the Father in My name, He will give it to you. Until now, you have asked nothing in My name. Ask, and you will receive, that your joy may be made full.

"I have spoken these things to you in figures of speech. But the time is coming when I will no more speak to you in figures of speech, but will tell you plainly about the Father. In that day you will ask in My name; and I don't say to you, that I will pray to the Father for you, for the Father Himself loves you, because you have loved Me, and have believed that I came forth from God. I came out from the Father, and have come into the world. Again, I leave the world, and go to the Father."

His disciples said to Him, "Behold, now You speak plainly, and speak no figures of speech. Now we know that You know all things, and don't need for anyone to question you. By this we believe that You came forth from God."

Jesus answered them, "Do you now believe? Behold, the time is coming, yes, and has now come, that you will be scattered, everyone to his own place, and you will leave Me alone. Yet I am not alone, because the Father is with Me.

"I have told you these things, that in Me you may have peace. In the world you have tribulation; but be of good cheer! I have overcome the world."

JESUS PRAYS FOR HIMSELF,
HIS DISCIPLES, AND ALL BELIEVERS
John 17:1-26

Jesus said these things, and lifting up His eyes to Heaven, He said, "Father, the time has come. Glorify Your Son, that Your Son may also glorify You; even as You gave Him authority over all flesh, He will give eternal life to all whom You have given Him. This is eternal life, that they should know You, the only true God, and Him Whom You sent, Jesus Christ. I glorified You on the earth. I have accomplished the work which You have given Me to do. Now, Father, glorify Me with Your own self with the glory which I had with You before the world existed.

"I revealed Your name to the people whom You have given Me out of the world. They were Yours, and You have given them to Me. They have kept Your word. Now they have known that all things whatever You have given Me are from You, for the words which You have given Me I have given to them, and they received them, and knew for sure that I came forth from You, and they have believed that You sent Me. I pray for them. I don't pray for the world, but for those whom You have given Me, for they are Yours. All things that are Mine are Yours, and Yours are Mine, and I am glorified in them. I am no more in the world, but these are in the world, and I am coming to You. Holy Father, keep them through Your name which You have given Me, that they may be one, even as We are. While I was with them in the world, I kept them in Your name. Those whom You have given Me I have kept. None of them is lost, except the son of perdition, that the Scripture might be fulfilled. But now I come to you, and I say these things in the world, that they may have My joy made full in themselves. I have given them Your word. The world hated them, because they are not of the world, even as I am not of the world. I pray not that You would take them from the world, but that You would keep them from the evil one. They are not of the world even as I am not of the world. Sanctify them in Your truth. Your word is truth. As You sent Me into the world, even so I have sent them into the world. For their sakes I sanctify Myself, that they themselves also may be sanctified in truth.

"Not for these only do I pray, but for those also who believe in Me through their word, that they may all be one; even as You, Father, are in Me, and I in You, that they also may be one in Us; that the world may believe that You sent Me. The glory which You have given Me, I have given to them; that they may be one, even as We are one; I in them, and You in Me, that they may be perfected into one; that the world may know that You sent Me, and loved them, even as You loved Me.

"Father, I desire that they also whom You have given Me be with Me where I am, that they may see My glory, which You have given Me, for You loved Me before the foundation of the world.

"Righteous Father, the world hasn't known You, but I knew You; and these knew that You sent Me. I made known to them Your name, and will make it known; that the love with which You loved Me may be in them, and I in them."

SECOND PREDICTION OF PETER'S DENIAL
Matthew 26:30-35; Mark 14:26-31; Luke 22:39-40a; John 18:1

When Jesus had spoken these words and when they had sung a hymn, He went out with His disciples over the brook Kidron, to the Mount of Olives where was a garden, into which He and His disciples entered as His custom was.

When He was at the place, then Jesus said to them, "All of you will be made to stumble because of Me tonight, for it is written,

'I will strike the shepherd, and the sheep of the flock will be scattered.'

"But after I am raised up, I will go before you into Galilee."

But Peter answered Him, "Even if all will be made to stumble because of You, I will never be made to stumble. Although all will be offended, yet I will not."

Jesus said to him, "Most assuredly I tell you that tonight, before the cock crows twice, you will deny Me three times."

Peter said to Him and spoke all the more, "Even if I must die with You, I will not deny You." All of the disciples also said likewise.

JESUS' AGONY IN THE GARDEN
Matthew 26:36-46; Mark 14:32-42; Luke 40b-46

Then Jesus came with them to a place called Gethsemane, and said to His disciples, "Sit here, while I go there and pray." He also said to them, "Pray that you don't enter into temptation."

He took with Him Peter and James, and John, the two sons of Zebedee, and began to be sorrowful, severely troubled, and distressed. Then He said to them, "My soul is exceedingly sorrowful, even to death. Stay here, and watch with Me."

He was withdrawn from them about a stone's throw, and He knelt down and fell on His face, and prayed, saying, "Abba, My Father, all things are possible to You, if You are willing and if it is possible, remove this cup from Me. Nevertheless, not My will, but Yours, be done." An angel from Heaven appeared to Him, strengthening Him.

Being in agony He prayed more earnestly. His sweat became like great drops of blood falling down on the ground. When He rose up from His prayer, He came to the disciples, and found them sleeping because of grief, and said to them and Peter, "Simon, are you sleeping? What, couldn't you watch with Me for one hour? Why do you sleep? Rise, watch, and pray that you may not enter into temptation. The spirit indeed is willing, but the flesh is weak."

Again, a second time He went away, and prayed, saying, "My Father, if this cup can't pass away from Me unless I drink it, Your will be done."

He came again and found them sleeping, for their eyes were heavy and they didn't know what to answer Him. He left them again, went away, and prayed a third time, saying the same words.

Then He came to His disciples, and said to them, "Sleep on now, and take your rest. It is enough. Behold, the hour is at hand, and the Son of Man is betrayed into the hands of sinners.

Arise, let us be going. Behold, he who betrays Me is at hand."

JESUS IS BETRAYED, ARRESTED AND FORSAKEN
Matthew 26:47-56; Mark 14:43-52; Luke 22:47-54; John 18:2-12

Now Judas, who betrayed Him, also knew the place, for Jesus often resorted there with His disciples. Judas then, having taken a detachment of soldiers and officers from the Chief Priests and the Pharisees, came there with lanterns, torches, and weapons.

While Jesus was still speaking, behold, a great multitude came with swords and clubs, from the Chief Priests , the Scribes, and Elders of the people, and he who was called Judas, one of the twelve, was leading them.

Jesus therefore, knowing all the things that were happening to Him, went forth, and said to them, "Who are you looking for?"

They answered Him, "Jesus of Nazareth."

Jesus said to them, "I AM." Judas also, who betrayed Him, was standing with them. When therefore He said to them, "I AM," they went backward, and fell to the ground.

Again therefore He asked them, "Who are you looking for?"

They said, "Jesus of Nazareth."

Jesus answered, "I told you that I AM. If therefore you seek Me, let these go their way," that the word might be fulfilled which He spoke, "Of those whom You have given Me, I have lost none."

Judas came near to Jesus to kiss Him because he who betrayed Him gave them a sign, saying, "Whoever I kiss, He is the One. Seize Him and lead Him away safely." Immediately he came to Jesus, and said, "Hail, Rabbi! Rabbi!" and kissed Him.

But Jesus said to him, "Friend, why are you here? Judas, do you betray the Son of Man with a kiss?" Then they came and laid hands on Jesus, and took Him.

When those who were around Him saw what was about to happen, they said to Him, "Lord, shall we strike with the sword?"

Simon Peter therefore, having a sword, drew it, and struck the high priest's servant, and cut off his right ear. The servant's name was Malchus.

But Jesus answered and said to Peter, "Put the sword into its sheath for all those who take the sword will die by the sword. The cup which the Father has given Me, shall I not surely drink it? Or do you think that I couldn't ask My Father, and He would even now send Me more than twelve legions of angels? How then would the Scriptures be fulfilled that it must be so? Let Me at least do this" -- and He touched his ear, and healed him.

In that hour Jesus said to the multitudes, and the Chief Priests , captains of the temple, and Elders, who had come against Him, "Have you come out as against a robber, with swords and clubs to seize Me? When I was with you and sat in the temple daily teaching, you didn't stretch out your hands against Me or arrest Me. But this is your hour, and the power of darkness. But all this has happened, that the Scriptures of the prophets might be fulfilled."

Then all the disciples left Him, and fled. A certain young man followed Him, having a linen cloth thrown around himself, over his naked body. The young men grabbed him, but he left the linen cloth, and fled from them naked.

So the detachment, the commanding officer, and the officers of the Jews, seized Jesus and bound Him. They led Him away, and brought Him into the high priest's house. But Peter followed from a distance.

FIRST JEWISH PHASE, BEFORE ANNAS
PETER BEGINS TO DENY JESUS
John 18:13-24

They then led Him to Annas first, for he was father-in-law to Caiaphas, who was high priest that year. Now it was Caiaphas who advised the Jews that it was expedient that one man should perish for the people.

Simon Peter followed Jesus, as did another disciple. Now that disciple was known to the high priest, and entered in with Jesus into the court of the high priest; but Peter was standing at the door outside. So the other disciple, who was known to the high priest, went out and spoke to her who kept the door, and brought in Peter.

Then the maid who kept the door said to Peter, "Are you also one of this Man's disciples?"

He said, "I am not."

Now the servants and the officers were standing there, having made a fire of coals, for it was cold. They were warming themselves. Peter was with them, standing and warming himself.

The high priest therefore asked Jesus about His disciples, and about His teaching.

Jesus answered him, "I spoke openly to the world. I always taught in synagogues, and in the temple, where the Jews always meet. I said nothing in secret. Why do you ask Me? Ask those who have heard Me what I said to them. Behold, these know the things which I said."

When He had said this, one of the officers standing by slapped Jesus with his hand, saying, "Do You answer the high priest like that?"

Jesus answered him, "If I have spoken evil, testify of the evil; but if well, why do you beat Me?" Annas sent Him bound to Caiaphas, the high priest.

SECOND JEWISH PHASE, BEFORE CAIAPHAS AND THE SANHEDRIN
Matthew 26:57-68; Mark 14:53-65

Then those who had taken Jesus led Him away to Caiaphas the high priest, where the Chief Priests , Scribes and the Elders were gathered together with Him. But Peter followed Him from a distance, to the court of the high priest, and entered in and sat with the officers to see the end. **He was warming himself in the light of the fire.**

Now the Chief Priests , the Elders, and the whole council sought false testimony against Jesus, that they might put Him to death; and they found none. Even though many false witnesses came forward, they found none. **Those who did come forward,** their testimony didn't agree with each other.

But at last two false witnesses came forward, stood up, and gave false testimony against Him. **They** said, "We heard Him say, 'I am able to destroy the temple of God that is made with hands, and to build it in three days without hands.'" Even so, their testimony did not agree.

The high priest stood up in the midst, and said to Him, "Have You no answer? What is this that these testify against You?" But Jesus held His peace, stayed quiet, and answered nothing.

The high priest answered Him, "I adjure You by the living God, that You tell us whether You are the Christ, the Son of God, the Son of the Blessed?"

Jesus said to him, "I AM. You have said it. Nevertheless, I tell you, henceforth you will see the Son of Man sitting at the right hand of Power, and coming on the clouds of Heaven."

Then the high priest tore his clothing, saying, "He has spoken blasphemy! Why do we need any more witnesses? Behold, now you have heard His blasphemy. What do you think?"

They all condemned Him to be worthy of death. They answered **him,** "He is worthy of death!"

Then they spit in His face and **covered** His face, and beat Him with their fists, and some slapped Him, saying, "Prophesy to us, You Christ! Who hit You?" The

143

officers struck Him with the palms of their hands.

PETER DENIES JESUS
Matthew 26:69-75; Mark 14:66-72; Luke 22:55-65; John 18:25-27

When they had kindled a fire in the middle of the courtyard below, and had sat down together, Peter sat among them. Now Simon Peter was standing and warming himself. A certain servant girl, a maid of the high priest, saw him as he sat in the light warming himself, and looking intently at him, said, "You aren't also one of His disciples, are you? You were also with Jesus the Nazarene, the Galilean!" She then said to those there, "This man also was with Him."

He denied Jesus before them all, saying, "I am not. Woman, I don't know Him. I don't know what you are talking about." He went out on the porch, and the cock crowed.

After a little while, when he had gone out onto the porch, someone else saw him, and said to him and to those who were there, "You also are one of them! This man also was with Jesus of Nazareth."

Again he denied it with an oath, and answered, "Man, I am not! I don't know the Man."

After about one hour passed, another one of the servants of the high priest, being a relative of him whose ear Peter had cut off recognized Peter and said, "Didn't I see you in the garden with Him?" He confidently affirmed this and those who stood by came and said to Peter, "Surely you are also one of them, for your speech makes you known. Truly this man also was with Him, for he is a Galilean!"

Peter therefore denied it again, and began to curse and to swear, saying, "I don't know the Man of Whom you speak! Man, I don't know what you are talking about!" Immediately, while he was still speaking, a rooster crowed the second time. The Lord turned, and looked at Peter. Then Peter remembered the Lord's word, how He said to him, "Before the rooster crows twice, you will deny Me three times." When he thought about that, he went out, and wept bitterly.

The men who held Jesus mocked Him and beat Him. Having blindfolded Him, they struck Him on the face and asked Him, "Prophesy! Who is the one who struck you?" They spoke many other things against Him, insulting Him.

THIRD JEWISH PHASE, BEFORE THE SANHEDRIN
Matthew 27:1; Mark 15:1a; Luke 22:66-71

Now when morning had come, as soon as it was day, the assembly of the Elders of the people were gathered together, both Chief Priests and Scribes, and the whole council, and they took counsel against Jesus to put Him to death: They led Him away into their council, saying, "If You are the Christ, tell us."

But He said to them, "If I tell you, you won't believe, and if I ask, you will in no way answer Me or let Me go. From now on, the Son of Man will be seated at the right hand of the power of God."

They all said, "Are You then the Son of God?"

He said to them, "You say it, because I AM."

They said, "Why do we need any more witness? For we ourselves have heard from His own mouth!"

THE REMORSE AND SUICIDE OF JUDAS
Matthew 27:3-10

Then Judas, who betrayed Him, when he saw that Jesus was condemned, felt remorse, and brought back the thirty pieces of silver to the Chief Priests and Elders, saying, "I have sinned in that I betrayed innocent blood."

But they said, "What is that to us? You see to it."

He threw down the pieces of silver in the sanctuary, and departed. He went away and hanged himself.

The Chief Priests took the pieces of silver, and said, "It's not lawful to put them into the treasury, since it is the price of blood." They took counsel, and bought the potter's field with them, to bury strangers in. Therefore that field was called "The Field of Blood" to this day. Then that which was spoken through Jeremiah the prophet was fulfilled, saying,

> "They took the thirty pieces of silver,
> the price of Him upon Whom a price had been set,
> Whom some of the children of Israel priced,
> and they gave them for the potter's field,
> as the Lord commanded me."

FIRST ROMAN PHASE, BEFORE PILATE
Matthew 27:2,11-14; Mark 15:1b-5; Luke 23:1-5; John 18:28-38

It was early, and they bound Him, and the whole company of them rose up and led Him away from Caiaphas into the Praetorium, and brought Him before Pontius Pilate, the governor. Yet they themselves didn't enter into the Praetorium, that they might not be defiled, but might eat the Passover.

Pilate therefore went out to them, and said, "What accusation do you bring against this man?"

They began to accuse Him, saying, "If this man weren't an evildoer, we wouldn't have delivered Him up to you. We found this man perverting the nation, forbidding paying taxes to Caesar, and saying that He Himself is Christ, a king."

Pilate therefore said to them, "Take Him yourselves, and judge Him according to your law."

Therefore the Jews said to him, "It is not lawful for us to put anyone to death," that the word of Jesus might be fulfilled, which He spoke, signifying by what kind of death He should die.

Pilate therefore entered again into the Praetorium, called Jesus, and **asked Him, "Are You the King of the Jews?"**

He answered him, "So you say. Do you say this by yourself, or did others tell you about Me?"

Pilate answered, "I'm not a Jew, am I? Your own nation and the Chief Priests delivered You to me. What have You done?"

Jesus answered, "My Kingdom is not of this world. If My Kingdom were of this world, then My servants would fight, that I wouldn't be delivered to the Jews. But now My Kingdom is not from here."

Pilate therefore said to Him, "Are You a king then?"

Jesus answered, "You say that I am a king. For this reason I have been born, and for this reason I have come into the world, that I should testify to the truth. Everyone who is of the truth listens to My voice."

Pilate said to Him, "What is truth?"

When he had said this, he went out again to the Jews, and said to **the Chief Priests and the multitudes, "I find no basis for a charge against this man."**

But they insisted, saying, "He stirs up the people, teaching throughout all Judea, beginning from Galilee even to this place."

When He was accused by the Chief Priests and Elders, He answered nothing. Then Pilate said to Him, "Have You no answer? Don't You hear how many things they testify against You?"

He gave him no answer, not even one word, so that the governor marveled greatly.

SECOND ROMAN PHASE, BEFORE HEROD
Luke 23:6-12

But when Pilate heard Galilee mentioned, he asked if the man was a Galilean. When he found out that He was in Herod's jurisdiction, he sent Him to Herod, who was also in Jerusalem during those days.

Now when Herod saw Jesus, he was exceedingly glad, for he had wanted to see Him for a long time, because he had heard many things about Him. He hoped to see some miracle done by Him. He questioned Him with many words, but He gave no answers. The Chief Priests and the Scribes stood, vehemently accusing Him. Herod with his soldiers humiliated Him and mocked Him. Dressing Him in luxurious clothing, they sent Him back to Pilate. Herod and Pilate became friends with each other that very day, for before that they were enemies with each other.

THIRD ROMAN PHASE, BEFORE PILATE AGAIN
Matthew 27:15-26; Mark 15:6-15; Luke 23:13-25; John 18:39-19:16

Pilate called together the Chief Priests and the rulers and the people, and said to them, "You brought this man to me as one that perverts the people, and see, I have examined Him before you, and found no basis for a charge against this man concerning those things of which you accuse Him. Neither has Herod, for I sent you to him, and see, nothing worthy of death has been done by Him. But you have a custom, that I should release someone to you at the Passover. Therefore do you want me to release to you the King of the Jews? I will therefore chastise Him and release Him."

Now at the feast the governor was accustomed to release to the multitude one prisoner, whom they desired. When therefore they were gathered together, Pilate said to them, "Whom do you want me to release to you? Barabbas, or Jesus, Who is called Christ?" For he knew that because of envy they had delivered Him up.

Now there was one called Barabbas who was a notable prisoner, bound with those who had made insurrection. He was a robber and one who was thrown into prison for a certain revolt in the city, and for murder. But he had to release one prisoner to them at the feast. Then they all shouted and cried out together, saying, "Not this man, but Barabbas! Away with this man! Release to us Barabbas!"

He said to them the third time, "Why? What evil has this man done? I have found no capital crime in Him. I will therefore chastise Him and release Him."

While he was sitting on the judgment seat, his wife sent to him, saying, "Have nothing to do with that righteous man, for I have suffered many things this day in a dream because of Him." Now the Chief Priests and the Elders persuaded the multitudes to ask for Barabbas, and destroy Jesus.

So Pilate then took Jesus, and flogged Him. The soldiers twisted thorns into a crown, and put it on His head, and dressed Him in a purple garment. They kept saying, "Hail, King of the Jews!" and they kept slapping Him.

Then Pilate went out again, and said to them, "Behold, I bring Him out to you, that you may know that I find no basis for a charge against Him." Jesus therefore came out, wearing the crown of thorns and the purple garment. Pilate said to them, "Behold, the man!"

Then Pilate spoke to them again, "Which of the two do you want me to release to you? Do you want me to release to you the King of the Jews?" He was still wanting to release Jesus.

The Chief Priests stirred up the multitude, that he should release Barabbas to them instead. **Then** the Chief Priests and the officers, **when they** saw Him, they shouted, saying, "Release to us Barabbas!"

Pilate said to them, "What then shall I do to Jesus, Who is called Christ? **The** one Whom you call the King of the Jews?"

They all said to him, "Let Him be crucified! Crucify! Crucify Him!"

But the governor said, "Why? What evil has He done?"

But they cried out exceedingly, saying, "Let Him be crucified!"

Pilate said to them, "Take Him yourselves, and crucify Him, for I find no basis for a charge against Him."

The Jews answered him, "We have a law, and by our law He ought to die, because He made Himself the Son of God."

When therefore Pilate heard this saying, he was more afraid. He entered into the Praetorium again, and said to Jesus, "Where are You from?" But Jesus gave him no answer. Pilate therefore said to Him, "Aren't You speaking to me? Don't You know that I have power to release You, and have power to crucify You?"

Jesus answered, "You would have no power at all against Me, unless it were given to you from above. Therefore he who delivered Me to you has greater sin."

At this, Pilate was seeking to release Him, but the Jews cried out, saying, "If you release this man, you aren't Caesar's friend! Everyone who makes himself a king speaks against Caesar!"

When Pilate therefore heard these words, he brought Jesus out, and sat down on the judgment seat at a place called "The Pavement," but in Hebrew, "Gabbatha." Now it was the Preparation Day of the Passover, at about the sixth hour. He said to the Jews, "Behold, your King!"

They cried out, "Away with Him! Away with Him! Crucify Him!" Pilate said to them, "Shall I crucify your King?" The Chief Priests answered, "We have no king but Caesar!"

But they were urgent with loud voices, asking that He might be crucified. So when Pilate saw that nothing was being gained, but rather that a disturbance was starting, he took water, and washed his hands before the multitude, saying, "I am innocent of the blood of this righteous person. You see to it."

All the people answered, "May His blood be on us, and on our children!"

Their voices and the voices of the Chief Priests prevailed. Pilate decreed that what they asked for should be done. He released to them Barabbas, who had been thrown into prison for insurrection and murder, for whom they asked, but he delivered Jesus up to their will to be crucified.

So they took Jesus and led Him away.

MOCKERY BY THE ROMAN SOLDIERS
Matthew 27:27-30; Mark 15:16-19

Then the governor's soldiers took Jesus into the Praetorium within the court, and gathered the whole garrison together against Him. They stripped Him, and put a scarlet purple robe on Him. They braided a crown of thorns and put it on His head, and a reed in His right hand; and they kneeled down before Him and began to salute Him, and mocked Him, saying, "Hail, King of the Jews!" They spat on Him, and took the reed and struck Him on the head and bowing their knees, did homage to Him.

JOURNEY TO GOLGOTHA
Matthew 27:31-34; Mark 15:20-23; Luke 23:26-33a; John 19:17

When they had mocked Him, they took the purple robe off of Him, and put His clothes on Him, and led Him away to crucify Him. He went out, bearing His cross, to the place called "The Place of a Skull," which is called in Hebrew, "Golgotha."

When they led Him away, they grabbed one Simon of Cyrene the father of Alexander and Rufus, who was passing by, coming from the country, and they compelled him to go with them, and laid on him the cross, to carry it after Jesus.

A great multitude of the people followed Him, including women who also mourned and lamented Him.

But Jesus, turning to them, said, "Daughters of Jerusalem, don't weep for Me, but weep for yourselves and for your children. For behold, the days are coming in which they will say, 'Blessed are the barren, the wombs that never bore, and the breasts that never nursed.' Then they will begin to tell the mountains, 'Fall on us!' and to the hills, 'Cover us.' For if they do these things in the green tree, what will be done in the dry?"

There were also others, two criminals, led with Him to be put to death.

When they came to the place called Golgotha, which is, being interpreted, 'The place of a skull,' they gave Him sour wine to drink mixed with gall and myrrh. When He had tasted it, He would not drink.

FIRST THREE HOURS ON THE CROSS
Matthew 27:35-44; Mark 15:24-32; Luke 23:33b-43; John 19:18-27

When they crucified Him there with the criminals, one on the right and the other on the left and the Scripture was fulfilled, which says,

"He was numbered with transgressors."

Jesus said, "Father, forgive them, for they don't know what they are doing."

Then the soldiers, when they had crucified Jesus, took His garments and made four parts, to every soldier a part; and also the coat. Now the coat was without seam, woven from the top throughout. Then they said to one another, "Let's not tear it, but cast lots for it to decide whose it will be," that the Scripture might be fulfilled, which says,

> "They parted My garments among them.
> For My cloak they cast lots."

Therefore the soldiers did these things. Dividing His garments among them, they cast lots to determine what each should take.

The people stood watching. The rulers with them also scoffed at Him, saying, "He saved others. Let Him save Himself, if this is the Christ of God, His chosen one!" Those who passed by blasphemed Him, wagging their heads, and saying, "Ha! You who destroy the temple, and build it in three days, save Yourself! If You are the Son of God, come down from the cross!"

Likewise the Chief Priests also mocking among themselves, with the Scribes, the Pharisees, and the Elders, said, "He saved others, but He can't save Himself. Let the Christ, if He is the King of Israel, let Him come down from the cross now, and we will believe in Him. He trusts in God. Let God deliver Him now, if He wants Him; for He said, 'I am the Son of God.'" The robbers also who were crucified with Him cast on Him the same reproach and insulted Him. The soldiers also mocked Him, coming to Him and offering Him vinegar, and saying, "If You are the King of the Jews, save Yourself!"

Pilate wrote a title also in letters of Greek, Latin, and Hebrew and put it on the cross: "JESUS OF NAZARETH, THIS IS THE KING OF THE JEWS." Therefore many of the Jews read this title, for the place where Jesus was crucified was near the city; The Chief Priests of the Jews therefore said to Pilate, "Don't write, 'The King of the Jews,' but, 'he said, I am King of the Jews.'"

Pilate answered, "What I have written, I have written."

But there were standing by the cross of Jesus His mother, and His mother's sister, Mary the wife of Clopas, and Mary Magdalene. Therefore when Jesus saw His mother, and the disciple whom He loved standing there, He said to His mother, "Woman, behold your son!" Then He said to the disciple, "Behold, your mother!" From that hour, the disciple took her to his own home.

One of the criminals who was hanged insulted Him, saying, "If You are the Christ, save Yourself and us!"

But the other answered, and rebuking him said, "Don't you even fear God, seeing you are under the same condemnation? And we indeed justly, for we receive the due reward for our deeds, but this man has done nothing wrong." He said to Jesus, "Lord, remember me when You come into Your Kingdom."

Jesus said to him, "Assuredly I tell you, today you will be with Me in Paradise."

THE LAST THREE HOURS ON THE CROSS
Matthew 27:45-50; Mark 15:33-37; Luke 23:44-45a,46; John 19:28-30

It was now about the sixth hour, and darkness came over the whole land until the ninth hour. About the ninth hour Jesus cried with a loud voice, saying, "Eli, Eli, lima sabachthani?" That is, "My God, My God, why have You forsaken Me?"

Some of them who stood there, when they heard it, said, "Behold, this man is calling Elijah."

Immediately one of them ran, and took a sponge, and filled it with vinegar, and put it on a reed, and gave Him a drink. The rest said, "Let Him be. Let's see whether Elijah comes to save Him and to take Him down."

After this, Jesus, seeing that all things were now finished, that the Scripture might be fulfilled, said,

"I am thirsty."

Now a vessel full of vinegar was set there; so they put a sponge full of the vinegar on hyssop, and held it at His mouth. When Jesus therefore had received the vinegar, He said, "It is finished."

Jesus then, crying with a loud voice, said, "Father, into Your hands I commit My Spirit!" Having said this, He bowed His head, and gave up His Spirit, and He breathed His last.

THE WITNESSES TO JESUS' DEATH
Matthew 27:51-56; Mark 15:38-41; Luke 23:45b, 47-49

Behold, the veil of the temple was torn in two from the top to the bottom. The earth quaked and the rocks were split. The tombs were opened, and many bodies of the saints who had fallen asleep were raised; and coming out of the tombs after His resurrection, they entered into the holy city and appeared to many.

When the centurion who stood by opposite Him, and those who were with him watching Jesus; when they saw the earthquake, and saw what was done, and that He cried out like this and breathed His last, they feared exceedingly, and glorified God, saying, "Truly this man was the Son of God. Certainly this was a righteous man."

All the multitudes that came together to see this, when they saw the things that were done, returned home beating their breasts. All His acquaintances, and the many women who came up with Him to Jerusalem and had followed Him from Galilee and who had been serving Him, stood at a distance, watching these things. Among them were Mary Magdalene, Mary the mother of James the younger and Joses, and Salome; and the mother of the sons of Zebedee.

JESUS' DEATH CONFIRMED AND THE BODY TAKEN DOWN
Matthew 27:57-58; Mark 15:42-45; Luke 23:50-52; John 19:31-38

Therefore the Jews, because it was the Preparation Day, that is, the day before the Sabbath, so that the bodies wouldn't remain on the cross on the Sabbath (for that Sabbath was a special one), asked of Pilate that their legs might be broken, and that they might be taken away.

Therefore the soldiers came, and broke the legs of the first, and of the other who was crucified with Him; but when they came to Jesus, and saw that He was already dead, they didn't break His legs. However one of the soldiers pierced His side with a spear, and immediately blood and water came out. He who has seen has testified, and his testimony is true. He knows that he tells the truth, that you may believe. For these things happened, that the Scripture might be fulfilled,

"A bone of Him will not be broken."

Again another Scripture says,

"They will look on Him Whom they pierced."

After these things, when evening had come, behold, a rich man, named Joseph, being a disciple of Jesus, but secretly for fear of the Jews, who was a prominent member of the council, a good and righteous man (he had not consented to their counsel and deed), from Arimathaea, a city of the Jews, who was also waiting for the Kingdom of God: this man boldly went to Pilate, and asked for Jesus' body. Pilate marveled if He were already dead; and summoning the centurion, he asked him whether He had been dead long. When he found out from the centurion, Pilate gave him permission. He came therefore and took away His body.

JESUS' BODY IS PLACED IN THE TOMB
Matthew 27:59-60; Mark 15:46; Luke 23;53-54; John 19:39-42

Nicodemus, who at first came to Jesus by night, also, with Joseph, came bringing a mixture of myrrh and aloes, about a hundred pounds. So they, Joseph and Nicodemus, took Jesus' body. They took the body down, and wrapped it in a linen cloth with the spices, as the custom of the Jews is to bury.

It was the day of the Preparation, and the Sabbath was drawing near. Now in the place where He was crucified there was a garden. In the garden Joseph laid Him in his own new tomb that was cut in stone, where no one had ever been laid and he rolled a great stone to the door of the tomb. Then because of the Jews' Preparation Day (for the tomb was near at hand) they laid Jesus there.

THE GUARD AT THE TOMB
Matthew 27:61-66; Mark 15:47; Luke 23:55-56

The women, who had come with Him out of Galilee, followed after, and saw the tomb, and how His body was laid. Mary Magdalene was there, and the other Mary, the mother of Joses, sitting opposite the tomb saw where He was laid. They

152

returned, and prepared spices and ointments. On the Sabbath they rested according to the commandment.

Now on the next day, which was the day after the Preparation Day, the Chief Priests and the Pharisees were gathered together to Pilate, saying, "Sir, we remember what that deceiver said while He was still alive: 'After three days I will rise again.' Command therefore that the tomb be made secure until the third day, lest perhaps His disciples come at night and steal Him away, and tell the people, 'He is risen from the dead;' and the last deception will be worse than the first."

Pilate said to them, "You have a guard. Go, make it as secure as you can."

So they went with the guard and made the tomb secure, sealing the stone.

THE TOMB IS VISITED BY THE WOMEN
Matthew 28:1; Mark 16:1

Now after the Sabbath, as it began to dawn on the first day of the week, Mary Magdalene and the other Mary the mother of James, and Salome, came to see the tomb. They bought spices, that they might come and anoint Him.

THE STONE IS ROLLED AWAY
Matthew 28:2-4

Behold, there was a great earthquake, for an angel of the Lord descended from Heaven, and came and rolled away the stone from the door, and sat on it. His appearance was like lightning, and his clothing white as snow. For fear of him, the guards shook, and became like dead men.

THE TOMB IS FOUND EMPTY BY THE WOMEN
Matthew 28:5-8; Mark 16:2-8; Luke 24:1-8; John 20:1

Very early on the first day of the week, the sun had barely risen at early dawn, while it was still dark, Mary Magdalene and some others came to the tomb, bringing the spices which they had prepared. They were saying among themselves, "Who will roll away the stone from the door of the tomb for us?" for it was very big. Looking up, they found the stone rolled away from the tomb.

They entered in, and didn't find the Lord Jesus' body and they were greatly perplexed about this, but then they saw a young man sitting on the right side, dressed in a white robe, and they were amazed. Then two men stood by them in dazzling clothing. Becoming terrified, they bowed their faces down to the earth.

The angel answered the women, he said to them, "Don't be afraid, for I know that you seek Jesus, the Nazarene, Who has been crucified. Why do you seek the living among the dead? He isn't here, but is risen just like He said. Come, see the place where the Lord was lying. Remember what He told you when He was still in Galilee, saying that the Son of Man must be delivered up into the hands of sinful men, and be crucified, and the third day rise again? Go quickly and tell His disciples and Peter, 'He has risen from the dead, and behold, He goes before you

153

into Galilee; there you will see Him as He said to you.' Behold, I have told you."

They remembered His words, and they departed quickly from the tomb with fear, astonishment, and great joy, and ran to bring His disciples word. They said nothing to anyone; for they were afraid.

THE TOMB IS FOUND EMPTY BY PETER AND JOHN
Luke 24:9-12; John 20:2-10

The women returned from the tomb, and told all these things to the eleven, and to all the rest. Now they were Mary Magdalene, Joanna, and Mary the mother of James. The other women with them told these things to the apostles.

Therefore she, **Mary Magdalene,** ran and came to Simon Peter, and to the other disciple whom Jesus loved, and said to them, "They have taken away the Lord out of the tomb, and we don't know where they have laid Him!" These words seemed to them to be nonsense, and they didn't believe them.

But Peter got up and the other disciple went out and ran to the tomb. They both ran together. The other disciple outran Peter, and came to the tomb first. Stooping and looking in, he saw the strips of linen lying by themselves, yet he didn't enter in. Then Simon Peter came, following him, and entered into the tomb. He saw the linen cloths lying, and the cloth that had been on His head, not lying with the linen cloths, but rolled up in a place by itself. So then the other disciple who came first to the tomb also entered in, and he saw and believed. For as yet they didn't know the Scripture, that He must rise from the dead.

So the disciples then departed to their homes, wondering what had happened.

APPEARANCE TO MARY MAGDALENE
Mark 16:9-11; John 20:11-18

Now when He had risen early on the first day of the week, He appeared first to Mary Magdalene, from whom He had cast out seven demons.

Mary had returned to the tomb and was standing outside at the tomb weeping. So, as she wept, she stooped and looked into the tomb, and she saw two angels in white sitting, one at the head, and one at the feet, where the body of Jesus had lain. They told her, "Woman, why are you weeping?"

She said to them, "Because they have taken away my Lord, and I don't know where they have laid Him." When she had said this, she turned around and saw Jesus standing, and didn't know that it was Jesus.

Jesus said to her, "Woman, why are you weeping? Who are you looking for?"

She, supposing Him to be the gardener, said to Him, "Sir, if you have carried Him away, tell me where you have laid Him, and I will take Him away."

Jesus said to her, "Mary."

She turned and said to Him, "Rabboni!" which is to say, "Teacher!"

Jesus said to her, "Don't touch Me, for I haven't yet ascended to My Father; but go to My brothers, and tell them, 'I am ascending to My Father and your Father, to My God and your God.'"

Mary Magdalene came and told the disciples as they mourned and wept, that she had seen the Lord, and that He had said these things to her. When they heard that He was alive, and had been seen by her, they disbelieved.

APPEARANCES TO THE OTHER WOMEN
Matthew 28:9-10

Some of the women had separated from the others and as they went to tell His disciples, behold, Jesus met them, saying, "Rejoice!" They came and took hold of His feet, and worshiped Him. Then Jesus said to them, "Don't be afraid. Go tell My brothers that they should go into Galilee, and there they will see Me."

THE SOLDIER'S REPORT TO THE JEWISH AUTHORITIES
Matthew 28:11-15

Now while the women were going, behold, some of the guards came into the city, and told the Chief Priests all the things that had happened. When they were assembled with the Elders, and had taken counsel, they gave a large amount of silver to the soldiers, saying, "Say that His disciples came by night, and stole Him away while we slept. If this comes to the governor's ears, we will persuade him and make you free of worry."

So they took the money and did as they were told. This saying was spread abroad among the Jews, and continues until this day.

APPEARANCE ON THE ROAD TO EMMAUS
Mark 16:12-13; Luke 24:13-32

After these things He was revealed in another form to two of them, as they walked, on their way into the country.

Behold, as the two of them were going that very day to a village named Emmaus, which was sixty stadia from Jerusalem, they talked with each other about all of these things which had happened. It happened, while they talked and questioned together, that Jesus Himself came near, and went with them. But their eyes were kept from recognizing Him.

He said to them, "What are you talking about as you walk, and are sad?"

One of them, named Cleopas, answered Him, "Are You the only stranger in Jerusalem who doesn't know the things which have happened there in these days?"
He said to them, "What things?"

They said to Him, "The things concerning Jesus, the Nazarene, Who was a prophet mighty in deed and word before God and all the people; and how the Chief Priests and our rulers delivered Him up to be condemned to death, and crucified Him. But we were hoping that it was He Who would redeem Israel. Yes, and besides all this, it is now the third day since these things happened. Also, certain women of our company amazed us, having arrived early at the tomb; and when they didn't find His body, they came saying that they had also seen a vision of angels, who said that He was alive. Some of us went to the tomb, and found it just like the women had said, but they didn't see Him."

He said to them, "Foolish men, and slow of heart to believe in all that the prophets have spoken! Didn't the Christ have to suffer these things and to enter into His glory?" Beginning from Moses and from all the prophets, He explained to them in all the Scriptures the things concerning Himself.

They drew near to the village, where they were going, and He acted like He would go further. They urged Him, saying, "Stay with us, for it is almost evening, and the day is almost over." He went in to stay with them.

It happened, that when He had sat down at the table with them, He took the bread and gave thanks. Breaking it, He gave to them. Their eyes were opened, and they recognized Him, and He vanished out of their sight. They said one to another, "Weren't our hearts burning within us, while He spoke to us along the way, and while He opened the Scriptures to us?" They went away and told it to the rest. They didn't believe them, either.

THE REPORT BY THE TWO TO THE DISCIPLES
Luke 24:33-35

They rose up that very hour, returned to Jerusalem, and found the eleven gathered together, and those who were with them, saying, "The Lord is risen indeed, and has appeared to Simon!" They related the things that happened along the way, and how He was recognized by them in the breaking of the bread.

APPEARANCE TO THE TEN DISCIPLES
Luke 24:36-43; John 20:19-25

When therefore it was evening, on that day, the first day of the week, and when the doors were locked where the disciples were assembled, for fear of the Jews, Jesus came and stood in the midst of them. As the two men from the road to Emmaus were speaking, Jesus Himself stood among them, and said to them, "Peace be to you."

But they were terrified and filled with fear, and supposed that they had seen a spirit. He said to them, "Why are you troubled? Why do doubts arise in your hearts? See My hands and My feet, that it is truly Me. Touch Me and see, for a spirit doesn't have flesh and bones, as you see that I have."

When He had said this, He showed them His hands and His feet and His side. While they still didn't believe for joy, and wondered, He said to them, "Do you have anything here to eat?" They gave Him a piece of a broiled fish and some honeycomb. He took them, and ate in front of them.

The disciples therefore were glad when they saw the Lord.

Jesus therefore said to them again, "Peace be to you. As the Father has sent Me, even so I send you." When He had said this, He breathed on them, and said to them, "Receive the Holy Spirit! Whoever's sins you forgive, they are forgiven them. Whoever's sins you retain, they have been retained."

But Thomas, one of the twelve, called Didymus, wasn't with them when Jesus came. The other disciples therefore said to him, "We have seen the Lord!"

But he said to them, "Unless I see in His hands the print of the nails, and put my hand into His side, I will not believe."

APPEARANCE TO THE ELEVEN
Mark 16:14; John 20:26-31

Afterward He was revealed to the eleven themselves as they sat at the table, and He rebuked them for their unbelief and hardness of heart, because they didn't believe those who had seen Him after He had risen.

After eight days again His disciples were inside, and Thomas was with them. Jesus came, the doors being locked, and stood in the midst, and said, "Peace be to you."

Then He said to Thomas, "Reach here your finger, and see My hands. Reach here your hand, and put it into My side. Don't be unbelieving, but believing."

Thomas answered Him, "My Lord and my God!"

Jesus said to him, "Because you have seen Me, you have believed. Blessed are those who have not seen, and have believed."

Therefore Jesus did many other signs in the presence of His disciples, which are not written in this book; but these are written, that you may believe that Jesus is the Christ, the Son of God, and that believing you may have life in His name.

ANOTHER APPEARANCE TO THE DISCIPLES
PETER IS RESTORED
John 21:1-25

After these things, Jesus revealed Himself again to the disciples at the sea of Tiberias. He revealed Himself this way. Simon Peter, Thomas, called Didymus, Nathanael of Cana in Galilee, and the sons of Zebedee, and two others of His disciples were together. Simon Peter said to them, "I'm going fishing." They told him, "We are also coming with you." They immediately went out, and entered into the boat. That night, they caught nothing.

But when day had already come, Jesus stood on the beach, yet the disciples didn't know that it was Jesus.

Jesus therefore said to them, "Children, have you anything to eat?"

They answered Him, "No."

He said to them, "Cast the net on the right side of the boat, and you will find some." They cast it therefore, and now they weren't able to draw it in for the multitude of fish.

That disciple therefore whom Jesus loved said to Peter, "It's the Lord!" So when Simon Peter heard that it was the Lord, he wrapped his coat around him (for he was naked), and threw himself into the sea. But the other disciples came in the little boat (for they were not far from the land, but about two hundred cubits away), dragging the net full of fish. So when they got out on the land, they saw a fire of coals there, and fish laid on it, and bread.

Jesus said to them, "Bring some of the fish which you have just caught."

Simon Peter went up, and drew the net to land, full of great fish, one hundred fifty-three; and even though there were so many, the net wasn't torn. Jesus said to them, "Come and eat breakfast." None of the disciples dared inquire of Him, "Who are You?" knowing that it was the Lord. Then Jesus came and took the bread, gave it to them, and the fish likewise. This is now the third time that Jesus was revealed to His disciples, after He had risen from the dead.

So when they had eaten their breakfast, Jesus said to Simon Peter, "Simon, son of Jonah, do you love Me more than these?"

He said to Him, "Yes, Lord; You know that I love You."

He said to him, "Feed My lambs."

He said to him again a second time, "Simon, son of Jonah, do you love Me?"

He said to Him, "Yes, Lord; You know that I love You."

He said to him, "Tend My sheep."

He said to him the third time, "Simon, son of Jonah, do you love Me?"

Peter was grieved because He asked him the third time, "Do you love Me?" He said to Him, "Lord, You know everything. You know that I love You."

Jesus said to him, "Feed My sheep. Most assuredly I tell you, when you were young, you dressed yourself, and walked where you wanted to. But when you are old, you will stretch out your hands, and another will dress you, and carry you where you don't want to go."

Now He said this, signifying by what kind of death he would glorify God.